GOLD

Gilding History & Techniques

GOLD

Gilding History & Techniques

Kirsten Beuster

4880 Lower Valley Road, Atglen, Pennsylvania 19310

Acknowledgements

I would like to thank all those colleagues who helped in the formation of this book and supported it, and also to wish all readers much happiness and inspiration with this Art Academy book on the fascination of gold.

Original edition *Die Kunst-Akademie Faszination Gold Tradition - Anwendung - Gestaltung* from Englisch Verlag Gmbh, Wiesbaden 2006.
Translated by Dr. Edward Force, Central Connecticut State University

Photos: Frank Schuppelius; photos on pp. 15 and 20: Frédéric Lebas
Design: Achim Ferger
Photo credits: p. 12: Bildquelle and © The Trustees of the British Museum, London, 2006; p. 14: Bildquelle and © J. G. Eytzinger GmbH, Schwabach, 2006; p. 17: Bildquelle and © The National Gallery, London, 2006; p. 21: Bildquelle: akg-images/Erich Lessing, Berlin; p. 53: Bildquelle: akg-images/Schütze-Rodemann, Berlin; p. 55: Bildquelle: Herve\ Champollion. akg-images, Berlin; p. 57: Bildquelle: akg-images, Berlin; p. 58: Bildquelle and © Trinity College, Dublin, 2006; p. 87-c) VG-Bildkunst, Bonn, 2006; Bildquelle: akg-images, Berlin; pp. 89/99: Bildquelle: akg-images, Berlin; p. 98: Bildquelle: Herve\ Champollion/ akg-images, Berlin; p. 101: Bildquelle and © Bayrische Verwaltung der Staatlichen Schlöser, Gärten und Seen, Munich, 2006; p. 104: Bildquelle: akg-images, Berlin; p. 105: © VG-Bildkunst, Bonn, 2006, Bildquelle: Museum Ludwig, Cologne/Schenkung Ludwig.

Dedication

For Lukas and Gaby

Schiffer Books are available at special discounts for bulk purchases for sales promotions or premiums. Special editions, including personalized covers, corporate imprints, and excerpts can be created in large quantities for special needs. For more information contact the publisher:

Published by Schiffer Publishing Ltd.
4880 Lower Valley Road
Atglen, PA 19310
Phone: (610) 593-1777; Fax: (610) 593-2002
E-mail: Info@schifferbooks.com

For the largest selection of fine reference books on this and related subjects, please visit our web site at
www.schifferbooks.com
We are always looking for people to write books on new and related subjects. If you have an idea for a book please contact us at the above address.

This book may be purchased from the publisher.
Include $3.95 for shipping.
Please try your bookstore first.
You may write for a free catalog.

In Europe, Schiffer books are distributed by
Bushwood Books
6 Marksbury Ave.
Kew Gardens
Surrey TW9 4JF England
Phone: 44 (0) 20 8392-8585; Fax: 44 (0) 20 8392-9876
E-mail: info@bushwoodbooks.co.uk
Website: www.bushwoodbooks.co.uk
Free postage in the U.K., Europe; air mail at cost.

Designed by Mark David Bowyer
Type set in Zurich BT / Aldine721 BT

ISBN: 978- 0-7643-2872-5
Printed in China

Contents

Ready to Write a Book?

Are you fascinated by the paranormal? Do you turn the conversation at every dinner party toward the otherwordly? Are you ready to share all the stories you've heard, and to investigate further?

We're eagerly seeking authors to pen local ghost story books. If this idea appeals to you, we'd love to hear more. Email your book idea to:

info@schifferbooks.com or write to Acquisitions, Schiffer Publishing, Ltd. 4880 Lower Valley Rd., Atglen, PA 19310, or call 610-593-1777 to make an appointment to speak with an editor.

Foreword
The Magic of Gold

The noble material of gold has played a special role for mankind since the beginning of metalworking. The nimbus of gold, its Latin name aurum, meaning "gleam," has since then reflected all the longings and desires of mankind and symbolized the dualism of human character between light and darkness. Like scarcely any other metal, gold not only arouses desire, power, and greed, but at the same time reflects man's longing for transcendence and search for an illuminated, divine principle.

The ancient poet Pindar (518-446 B.C.) was already warning in the 5th century that gold was a child of Zeus that was not attacked by either time or rust, but consumed the soul of man. In Egypt, the god Aton was symbolized by a golden sun disc. Thus the sun, light, and gold possess a common quality that comes from their uncommon glowing power and has inspired mankind for generations. Augustus (354-300 B.C.) already differentiated between the glow and the radiance of the divine light—lux—and perceived light—lumen. The visible light seemed to him to be a depiction of God, a being of light, or a metaphysical symbol of truth. From this philosophical concept, the painting of the Middle Ages chose its gold backgrounds as a symbol of the divine light. The elements of gold and silver represented the true light of God, which set the portrayed angels, madonnas, and saints apart from the real world.

Polished, gleaming gold reflects light remarkably well and is often utilized in this sense. The brighter the surface, the more reflective effect its metallic gleam has. In the spectrum of light, gold is in the blue range before ultra-violet; thus its metallic glow appears to the human eye as the complementary color yellow. Through this "magic" glowing power, its permanence, its flexibility and its glitter, gold has for centuries been a symbol for power, beauty and spirituality.

In the realm of artistic handiwork, gold is a great challenge, for it sets not only the highest demands for precise workmanship, but also requires sensible application because of its colorful dominance. For only thriftily and deliberately applied gold can increase the formative or esthetic effect of an object. Here the greatest possible care, neatness, patience and precision in workmanship and application are required.

Every object to be gilded becomes unique and makes very individual demands on its workers. The art of gilding has scarcely changed for thousands of years. Its basic principles have remained unchanged from the times of the pharaohs to the present. Only the quality of the materials and the variety of the surfaces have changed over the centuries. Sensitive work with gold leaf cannot even today be equaled by machine work in its high artistic quality, for it demands not only a very high degree of handcrafting ability, but also experience. Thus this book can be only a brief guide to the basic concepts and a few techniques of gilding.

I hope all readers will, by the end of the book, share my enthusiasm for this sensitive and shining precious metal and develop many new inspirations for their own creations!

Much joy and success are wished you.

Chapter One
Cultural History of Gilding

The Material Gold

Gold is a precious metal and is represented by the abbreviation Au in the periodic table of chemical elements. Pure gold has a reddish-yellow color and is a very soft, stretchable material. Thus when it is worked, it is usually used in alloy form, with other metals mixed in.

Gold as a chemical element is very unreactive; as a rule; it is not attacked by acids and alkalines, and cannot oxidize in pure form. It dissolves only in a mixture of hydrochloric and nitric acids, in cyanide solutions or in hot concentrated sulfuric acid. A solution of gold in hydrochloric and nitric acids is called chlor-gold or gold chloride. It was used in the past, for example, in the fire-gilding of metal objects. Another variant is the so-called "gold purple", which is used in glass and porcelain painting and the production of ruby glass.

Gold occurs naturally in various forms: as fine sand or nuggets. In a very pure form, it is found in rivers and river sands, and is often found along with other metals in underground gold veins. To this day, it is unearthed by panning or mining. The most commonly found form occurs in veins in quartz rock. It is washed out by water and deposited in streams. Mined gold is often found along with other metals, such as silver, mercury, platinum or iron. The metals are separated by complicated technical and chemical processes. Gold is most commonly found mixed with silver.

In Egypt, rich gold deposits made the mining of it possible as early as 4100 B.C. Later, the Egyptians also imported their gold from distant places, such as South Africa. Herodotus of Halicarnassus (490-425 B.C.) mentions the antique obtaining of gold from the island of Siphnos, and describes how the Indians had to pay tribute in gold to the Persian King Darius. The writer Appianus of Alexandria (95-165 B.C.) described how gold was obtained in Colchis, on the shore of the Black Sea, by hanging sheepskins in the rivers.

The gold grains were caught in the tangled fleece and could be picked out later. Presumably, the ancient sags of the "Golden Fleece" found its origin here. In ancient times, the peninsula of Iberia supplied Europe with gold until the Romans exhausted the resources. The "Rheingold" of the Nibelungen saga also tells of central European gold acquisition in the distant past.

Many of these sources of gold have been lost; today the greatest sources of gold are in South Africa, North America, and Australia.

Carat Calculation & Gold Alloys

As a rule, gold is used in various combinations with other metals. It takes on a bright greenish coloring with added silver,, and a reddish cast with added copper. In this way, not only the color of gold, but also its characteristics, such as elasticity and ease of being worked, can be varied. The calculation of all additions in a gold alloy is reckoned in carats, or in newer practice, in thousandths (333, 585, 750, 980). The basis of the carat system is the "Cologne Mark," which was divisible into 24 parts (carats) and weighed 233.8 grams.

High- and low-carat types of gold are differentiated. 24-carat gold weighing 233.8 grams is pure gold, 1000 parts of 1000. 24-karat gold leave is usually used externally. Gold leaf is alloyed for various other uses. The types of gold vary from 24 to 6 carats, and can be had in numerous colors and percentages.

Carat Calculation

1 Cologne Mark = 24 carats	=	233.8 grams
1 carat in grams	=	9.7 grams
1 carat in thousandths	=	41.7/1000

Gold in various degrees of purity				
Designation	**Carats**	**Mixed with**	**Color**	**Use**
Three-crown gold	24	--	--	Exterior
Gold alloys in use				
Ducat gold	23	Silver/copper	yellowish	mainly interior
Red gold	23	Copper	reddish	mainly interior
Orange gold	22	Silver/copper	orange	interior
Gold with platinum	17	Platinum	reddish/silver	interior
Yellow gold	18	Silver	bright gold/silver	interior
Green gold	16.7	Silver	greenish/silver	interior
White gold	12 or 6	Silver	silver	interior

The Development of Gold Leaf Gilding

Work with sheet metals and the artistic handicraft of gilding were already practiced in the early high cultures, such as by the Babylonians, Persians, Egyptians, Mayas and Aztecs. Many traditions blended into the belief that the material of gold, because of its shimmer, its glitter and its many ways of being worked, contained something special or even godly. It was used for the most varied objects, such as jewelry, sacred articles or coins. It was also used to ennoble other materials, such as wood, textiles, glass, or book illumination.

Working with pure gold developed into the gilding of objects with gold sheet or leaf. These objects were at first covered with thick gold sheets, and later with gold leaf beaten thinner and thinner. Thinner gold leaf also allowed the gilding of complicated shapes. Through this development, gold leaf served to enhance the value of apparently less valuable materials, and in the course of history it projected its material aspects more and more into the foreground.

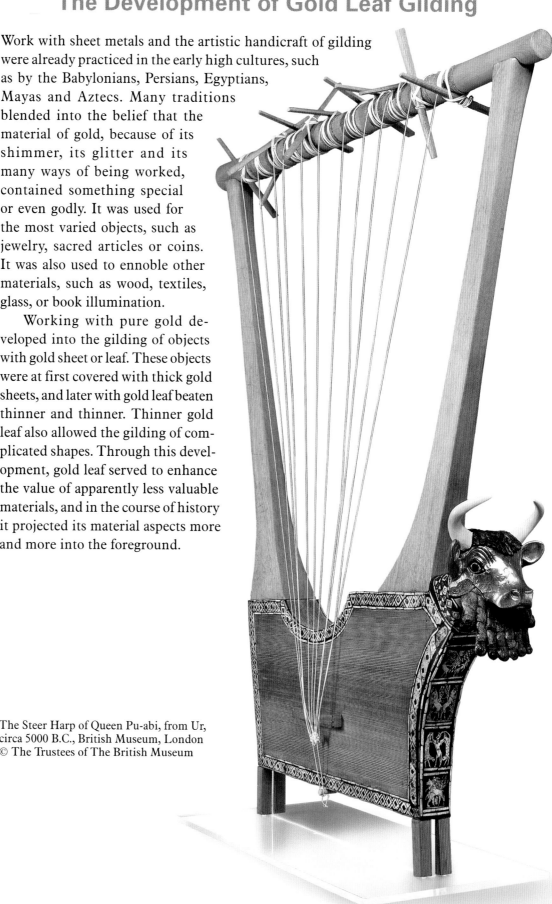

The Steer Harp of Queen Pu-abi, from Ur, circa 5000 B.C., British Museum, London
© The Trustees of The British Museum

In ancient times, the Roman historian Pliny the Elder (in his Naturalis Historia), in the first century A.D., already mentioned the ancient production of gold leaf. He named "synopsis." a clay of yellow ochre, at the background for gold-leaf gilding. The possibility of polishing the background was not yet mentioned.

In the Middle Ages, not only the Lucca Manuscript of the 9th century, but also the most important German manuscript, the Schedula diversarium atrium by Theophilus of Helmershausen, from the 12th century, describe many types of gold-leaf gilding. For example, the priming of a wooden table, the so-called "shooting" and the polishing with an animal tooth are described there. The techniques of gilding were also known to the monks of Mount Athos in the 13th century. In their painting book, the Hermeneia des Dionysos, such exotic materials for gilding as snail saliva and crushed garlic are mentioned, and for the first time, the techniques of present-day bole gilding are described.

In the 14th-century Trattato della Pittura by Cennino Cennini (1370-1440), the work of gilding in a medieval workshop is described. Giorgio Vasari (1511-1574) reports similarly. From these portrayals we can see that the painters first adopted the art of gilding, and that the two arts separated only in the 16th century. Since then the occupations of the painter and the gilder or "Fassmaler" (meaning a painter of objects) have been separate.

In the Renaissance, in the 16th century, the significance of gold changed. As a new aspect, the material of gold came into the foreground as a color and pure means of decoration. At this time, the separation of the picture and frame also occurred. The gold backgrounds gave way to the gilded frame, and the occupation of the frame-gilder arose. The fading of the churchly monopoly in working gold, the development of the bourgeois class, and the forming of guilds all helped to change the gilder's and gold-beater's handicraft from a purely clerical to a bourgeois craft.

In the 19th century, in the era of beginning industrialization, a new division of handicraft and industry took place. The classic handicraft lost importance to industrial production, which was developing quickly. The traditional handicraft with its individual formation competed with mass production in the making of frames and moldings. The production of gilded objects was changed again since the introduction of free trade (since 1810 in Prussia and 1868 in Bavaria) and the related dissolution of trade barriers. Various businesses adopted gilding as their own. This is true to this day, with very different uses and standards of quality. The occupation of the gilder, though, remained alive in small, fine work. To this day, even the most modern technology cannot equal the sensitivity and precision of the gilder in working with gold leaf.

The Production of Gold Leaf

In ancient Egypt, the art of gilding with thin rolled or beaten gold leaf had already reached a high point. Thus the early techniques of gold-leaf gilding were already known more than 2500 years ago. Very thin beaten gold leaf with a thickness of only 1/1000 mm was produced, to be equaled by German goldsmiths only in the 18th century.

The art of beating gold had changed only slightly since the antique cultures. Gold leaf is made for the most part by hand to this day, since there are no machines that could beat the gold to a thickness of 1/8000 to 1/10,000 mm.

For the production of gold leaf, molten gold is heated to 1200 degrees Celsius, poured out onto a stone called a "Zain," and after cooling, it is rolled into a metal strip. To keep the gold malleable, it is reheated from time to time. This is continued until the gold strip has reached a thickness of 1/33 mm. After that it is cut into squares,

so-called "quartiere". These are placed between parchment (the so-called "thick squeeze" of some 400 to 600 pieces) and beaten in an initial process with a hammer on a granite block. The parchment paper (also called goldbeater's skin) is made of leather waste, and thus can take great pressure. The gold leaves are now quartered and placed again between sheets of goldbeater's skin (the lot form). A lot consists of about 1300 leaves of parchment paper measuring 16 x 16 cm, and is struck again with the spring hammer.

The actual thin beating begins only now. The gold leaves are quartered again and beaten in several processes to a thickness of 1/1000 mm. In the last beating process, the gold leaves are dusted, so they do not stick, and finally beaten to a thickness of 1/8888 mm. The last process is done with a heavy hammer. The goldbeater usually delivers some 5000 strokes by hand.

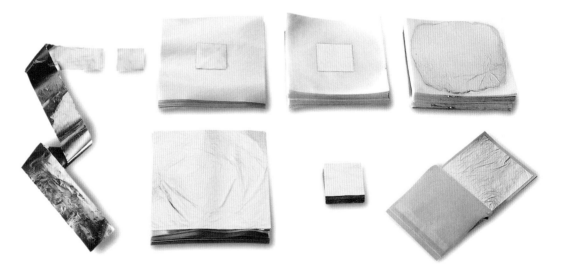

Gold leaf is beaten from a narrow strip of sheet gold into thinner and thinner leaves, until it finally reaches a thickness of 1/7000 to 1/10,000 mm.

The gold leaf now has a square shape of 13 to 15 cm. It is now cut manually by the gold cutter to the required size measuring 80 x 80 mm square, and each leaf is placed between silk paper in so-called "notebooks" of 25 leaves each. A "book" of gold, the customary trade unit, consists of 250 or 300 gold leaves. For external use, each individual leaf is also pressed onto fine silk paper. A difference is made with genuine gold leaf between transfer or storm gold for external use and loose gold leaf for internal use.

The Development of the Gold Frame

A "gold frame" is a frame, either gilded with gold leaf or painted, which was made in a goldsmith's workshop as a one-off piece for a picture or mirror. The development of the gold frame began as early as the 12th century. At this time, free-standing panels were used on altars, and over the years they were replaced by more and more lavish creations. From them there derived the movable altars of the 15th and 16th centuries. They were made by "painter-brushers" or "painter-artists," most of whom had some knowledge of gilding. Many woodcarvers, such as Master Bertram (1330-1415), made the facades and gilded them on their great carved altars, such as the high altar of St. Petri (also called the Grabow altar). The significance of the carved figures went back, through the deliberate use of unpainted carved-wood altars, to the woodcarvers Veit Stoss (1445-1533) or Tilman Riemenschneider (1460-1531).

In the 16th century, the "painters" and the "brushers" separated. The gold backgrounds disappeared, and the frame separated from the picture once and for all, becoming a separate object. The gold became primarily a coloring and decorating element, and lost part of its religious character. With the mounting of the pictorial forms on the walls, the link with a churchly location was lost, and the first new aspects of interior decoration appeared.

Carved altar segments of a carved ad gilded northern Spanish altar, circa 1545 by Alonso Bergruete. Bole gilding with varying rubbing and decorating techniques.

Frame creation developed from furniture building, and was hastened by the invention of the sawmill in the early 14th century. The first moldings and profiles for the production of frames could be produced, rationalizing the woodcarver's work. For the first framed pictures, in the 15th century, the artistic frames often were made of the same wood as the pictures themselves, and bore texts that referred to the pictures. The massive sacred altarpieces were finally replaced by thinner boards. Later, the wedge frame developed as the single carrier of a stretched linen picture. The art cabinet of the 16th century, in which many framed pictures were first presented in a single room as a formative total concept, preferred simpler frames.

Many historical gilding shops worked together with well-known architects, woodcarvers and other artistic artisans. Thus the gilders were often members of large workshops, and thus they were scarcely recognizable, with few exceptions. Often the gilders were wandering artisans from outside, and like the convent painters and court handcrafters, they were not bound to a guild, and carried out their work on new buildings, or created splendid structures to order.

Thus the individual signing of a picture frame was rare, and became customary only in the 18th century with the arrival of the "Ebenists" (highly specialized artistic cabinetmakers, who produced intarsia work). In barrel painting (the colorful painting of stone and wooden items, in which the gilding or the gilded areas were "closed in" by the colors), signatures are just as rarely found on the backs of figures. Some names or signatures, though, were set in cartouches or on slips of paper set into prepared altars.

The production of artistic frames or mirrors completed the making of picture frames, and showed that a frame could now serve as an independent object of art. Thus the frame developed into one of the most mobile of all artistic goods. Valuable frames were often reworked during the course of their history, their forms were copied or varied, and can thus be fitted into a concrete art-historical chronology only with difficulty.

The Gilder's Workshop
The studio of a frame gilder;
Encyclopedia of Diderot and
D'Alembert, Paris,
1751 and 1765.

Picture Frames—A Historical Overview

The first separate frames were made in the 15th century. Since ancient times, and in the Early Middle Ages, there were mainly textile pictures (such as on wall hangings) as mobile furnishings for private rooms. In ancient wall paintings, though, there were already picture areas, which were rimmed by ornamental friezes or edges. The first altar pictures, portable portraits of emperors on wooden or stone panels, pictures of ancestors or other portraits, were set up or hung in public places. These can be seen as forerunners of portable pictures and their frames.

Altar Frame Jacopo di Cione, The Crucifixion, tempera on wood, © The National Gallery, London. Bole gilding with etching, chasing and engraving techniques, plus inset vignettes.

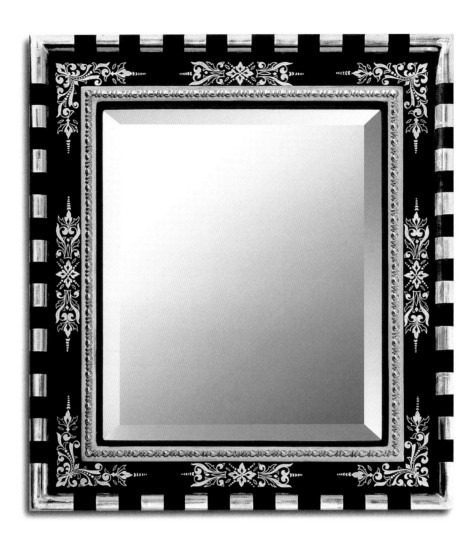

Frame in Renaissance Style
Alte Pinakothek,. Munich.
Yellow gold, bole gilding and
etching.

The medieval altarpieces were a vital part of church decoration. At this time, the pictures were already made three-dimensionally and built in architectural forms. From these elements taken from architecture and using connecting links, and the profiling of wall surfaces, there developed a separate form of the first independently made frames. In the churches, the architectural form, with or without gables, in a large altar design were called aedicular frames. The smaller forms of this type were called tabernacle frames.

This strictly organized form contrasted in the 15th century with the great circular Italian frames with endless decorative wreaths of fruit or leaves, which were called altar frames (figure, p. 17), and often adorned Madonnas, such as in the paintings of Raphael of Urbino (1483-1520). Various carved leaf frames with wide all-around profiles of acanthus leaves or plate frames with etched ornamentation are typical of the Italian Renaissance.

Opposite: Architectural frame in glittering and matte gold, with etched and decorative techniques.

From the Madonnas, portrait painting finally developed. Their frames formed a transition from clerical to laic themes. The patrons in the Renaissance were, besides the churches, increasing numbers of the nobility and bourgeoisie.

New frame forms with extending profile corners and curving contours, such as those of the Venetian Sansovino frames of the 16th century, with usually floral or classic-styled ornamentation.

These forms also continued into the Italian Baroque. The Hollanders, on the other hand, preferred simple black frames, veneered with ebony or tortoise-shell, and with partially glued flame or wave veneers, since the 17th century.

Along with them, fancy frames were widespread in the Baroque and Rococo eras as characteristic possessions of the ruling class. More and more of these frames stood out because of their three-dimensional dynamics and alternation of convex and concave forms, which were borrowed from the contemporary architecture. The introduction of various decorative techniques for frame surfaces put more stress on flat and three-dimensional ornamentation. This was achieved by decorative etched, engraved or chased techniques which are still used today.

Louis XIV Frame Bole gilding, decorated with fields and engraving.

In England, frames usually developed from Italian or French models, and a particularly well-developed variation is seen in the Chippendale frames of the 18th century (Thomas Chippendale, Sr., 1718-1779). These elegant craved frames united Rokoko forms with the arising Chinese and Neo-gothic styles. In the 19th century, art was reevaluated by the philosophy of the Awakening. Purpose-linked art was now strictly forbidden, and esthetics became all-important. In frame styling, there was a return to classically strict substantial forms.

The simplicity of the Biedermeier frames shows this clearly. The frames, like home interiors, were made of simple, light woods such as birch, and had black-colored or ebony intarsia corners as their only decorations.

Classicism developed from the new dependence on classic-historical forms, such as the thin pressed-on antique palmetto-leaf or tendril décor. Also typical were channelings carved into the background in the hollow areas of the picture frames, completed with acanthus-leaf corner decoration.

"Josef Pembaur" Gustav Klimt, 1890. Painted, engraved flat frame with matte bole gilding.

Top Left:
Historical Ornamentation
with an acanthus leaf as a
frame decoration.

Top Right:
Corinthian Capital with
channeling and acanthus-leaf
decoration.

This purity of esthetic form developed further in the subsequent Historicism, but the simplicity of the frame disappeared. The Classical repertory of forms from all preceding eras was taken up again and combined on wide, heavy frame profiles.

The following Art Nouveau, newly conceived out of organically marked forms, finally ended the conception that the frame had to have a striking, all-around pattern. Flat, simple frame profiles were often brought into a context shared with the picture itself. In this way, imaginative figural associations or calligraphic fields appeared on the frame profiles. Many artists, such as Gustav Klimt (1862-1918), used the frame and the gold material as integral parts of their art.

Present-day frames usually retain the spirit of the Bauhaus style of the twenties and thirties of the 20th century. The development of industrial series production pushed the theme of picture framing to a new level. Various metal frames, changeable frames and rimless picture carriers characterize the market today. The picture is a portable piece of furnishing which has a varying value in interior decorating. Many original pictures in oil or acrylic are fitted with only a simple shadow frame in the course of the new purism, or integrated into a modern interior without a frame at all.

The classically decorated frames find a home today principally in the shadow area, as portrait frames, or in the goldsmith's studio in the course of restoration and conservation. The tendency in modern frames in now toward simple, clear and restrained profiles in cool, silvery white gold or even platinum tones.

Frame based on Art Nouveau Bole gilding in white gold, with engraved ornamentation.

Opposite: Frame in Cubist Style Bole gilding, silver, engraved.

The Mirror Frame

Mirrors are among mankind's oldest utilitarian objects. The first mirrors are known from early antiquity. While in ancient Greece a mirror was usually made of bronze or silver, bronze mirrors covered with silver or platinum have survived from China.

In symbolic connection with the Narcissus myth, the mirror has been known since antiquity as a part of the soul, and the rippling of water into which someone looked meant danger for the soul. From this time came the present-day superstition that breaking a mirror brought bad luck. Especially blackened magic mirrors for the art of prophecy and soothsaying have been used since antique times. The fascinating phenomenon of the mirror and reflection has influenced and inspired philosophy, religion, science and art over the course of time. In gilding, the mirror frame is still one of the most creative means of handicraft and artistic expression.

In Venice at the beginning of the Renaissance, it first became possible to produce crystal and blown mirror glass, which replaced the old bronze, silver or tinplate mirrors. Since then, mirrors of all shapes and kinds have been set in suitable frames, and to make the reflections on their surfaces real for the observer. At the same time, the separation of picture and frame took place in painting, and the mirror frame became a widespread decorative and simultaneously mobile cultural object along with the picture.

Fancy mirrors of gold, silver, iron or crystal glass first appeared in the inventory lists of royal courts in the 15th and 16th centuries. Concave and convex mirror shapes were listed there as specialties.

In the 16th century, mirror manufacturers on the Italian island of Murano had a monopoly, and until the middle of the 17th century, almost all the crystal mirrors in Europe were produced there. From there, mirror production spread via Flanders and Germany into all of Europe, In the 17th century, the so-called "halls of mirrors," the most famous one of which was set up at Versailles under the "Sun King" Louis XIV (1643-1715).

The 19th century brought forth the so-called "Psyche," one of the first free-standing dressing mirrors, first designed and produced for the French Empress Josephine (1763-1814), the wife of Napoleon, and named in reference to the ancient myth of Narcissus.

In Art Nouveau and Art Deco, the mirror was often seen as a vital part of interior decoration, such as in the "Willow Tea Rooms" in Glasgow, made by Charles Rennie Macintosh (1868-1924).

In the 20th century, the mirror finally separated from its decorative frame in the developments at the Bauhaus and by Le Corbusier (1887-1965). Through the series production of modern industry, the ornamentation faded into the background, and the mirror advanced to become a purely functional and purely esthetic object.

Mirror frame with ornamental bow, in classicistic style. Matte white gold, with bole gilding in white gold.

Gilding Techniques

Two basic techniques of gilding are differentiated: chemical gilding and mechanical gilding.

The various types of chemical gilding are, with the exception of fire-gilding, all of recent origin. Fire-gilding consisted of applying to a prepared metal piece a gold-amalgam coating, of which the mercury it contained evaporated—and very toxic and subsequently banned process. Chemical gilding, though, reached its high point with galvanic gilding in an electrolytic bath, and with contact gilding.

Mechanical gilding is the oldest type of process. It generally consisted of plating objects with gold sheets. This process was already known to the high antique cultures, and is practiced to this day. The following techniques exist: Gloss and matte gilding, bole gilding, oil gilding, mordant gilding and gilding behind glass. According to the background material, they were suited to the object very individually, but always remained the same in their basic work processes.

The most frequent gilding techniques are matte oil gilding and high-gloss bole gilding. Mordant gilding (matte gilding on a wax surface) and polished white technique (a white polished treatment of sculptures) were used by churchly painters in the interior decoration of churches. In the realms of advertising and making coats of arms, gilding behind glass or otherwise was done by manuscript illuminators. The use of gold leaf on various metal surfaces, on architectural and other components, is carried out by the Gilder. On stone surfaces, such as tombstones, gilding is often done by stonemasons. Gilding on paper or leather is a basic part of present-day bookbinding, which completes the varied spectrum of gilding techniques.

Opposite: Frame based on Art Nouveau style. White gold, bole gilding and engraving work by Wiebke Schwerdtfeger.

Chapter Two
Surfaces, Tools, & Materials

The Surface

In this chapter, the most important tools, adhesives, chalks, lacquers and solvents for gilding will be described. They are part of the basic equipment in a gilding shop, and should in principle be on hand in small quantities, so that the appropriate gilding processes can be carried out.

In principle, gold leaf can be applied to almost any surface. This applies to organic surfaces, such as wood, plaster, stucco, linen, paper, fabrics and leather, as well as inorganic surfaces, such as metal, glass or stone. Gilding can also be done on modern synthetic materials.

To begin, the surface must be cleaned thoroughly. Rust, grease, and any paint already present must be removed, and the surface must then be checked thoroughly again for firmness and cleanliness, since the layers of color to be applied could not adhere otherwise. In addition, chemical or physical reactions between the surface and the gilding could occur if the surface is insufficiently prepared. Gilding is divided into outside and inside uses according to how it is used. The organic, traditional techniques of polimernt gloss gilding or mordant gilding are suitable only for interior use, since the classic construction with glue or wax adhesives is water-soluble. For outside use, gilding is usually applied on lacquered surfaces, as in oil gilding. No silver or white gold can be used outside, for these metals oxidize very quickly and are strongly attacked by acids and alkalines from the environment. For outside gilding, the purest gold is always used: 23.75- or 24-carat. The silver or white-gold tones can be replaced here by expensive palladium or platinum.

It is true of all surfaces that gold-leaf gilding can never be completely protected from external mechanical damage. This should be the main point of all further considerations in making a decision of whether an object is to be gilded. Many objects in everyday use, or objects that are exposed to regular mechanical demands, thus are not suitable for gold-leaf gilding. The gilding would not be sturdy or immune to scratching, and would also not be able to withstand the pressures, even with an expensive lacquer coating.

A Tip

Cleanliness is the highest law in all the following steps, since a dusty or greasy surface makes gilding impossible. The work bench, the needed tools and materials, as well as the surfaces, should thus be prepared carefully. This is the best protection from unpleasant later surprises or unsatisfactory results.

The Tools

The following tools are especially important for the gilder's handiwork. A basic assortment of various other woodworking tools and brushes is assumed. Various empty containers, a water bath, lint-free cloths and means of grinding complete the gilder's equipment.

The Spatula & Modeling Irons

This important utensil is a flat tool that tapers at both ends to become round, pointed, flat or oblong. Small spatulas or modeling irons (also called "Kitteisen") are used for modeling, filling of empty places, and many other tasks. They can also be made out of wood or taken from among the stucco worker's tools. Spatulas with handles, in various sizes, are also helpful for work on large surfaces.

The Engraving Hook

Engraving hooks are made of steel and set in wooden handles. They have variously curved blades and are either rounded, straight-edged or pointed at the front. The width of the blade can vary from 4 mm to 12 mm. These repairing tools are used for various decorating techniques, such as the artistic damask or brocade patterns, and for precise finishing of decorated forms.

The Punches

So-called punching irons are used for the technique of punching. Alternatively, iron or steel nails, with their undersides variously formed to make appropriate shapes when used in punching, can also be used. In the Middle Ages there were often gold backgrounds that were marked with points, rings, stars or diamonds. This technique, in which the tool is driven into the background with a hammer, ranks among the oldest decorative techniques in the history of gilding. Today there are several manufacturers who have included these classic punching forms in their programs again. Hollow, ball, line, mat and ornament punches are used. There is also a special little punching hammer with a curved, sprung handle, with which the punch is carefully driven into the background.

Punching iron with various patterns

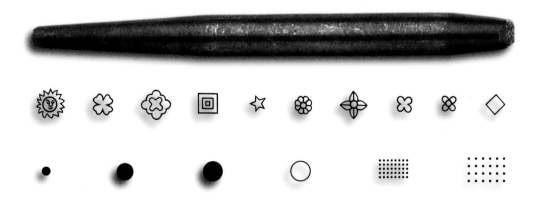

The Brushes

Good brushes are characterized by high elasticity of the bristles. Their so-called "natural end" is also vital. This means that their ends run together to form a point and do not turn away from each other. A good brush can take up a lot of paint and transport it without dripping. Synthetic brushes hold the paint les well than natural brushes, but they are sturdier.

It is essentially true that hair brushes are better suited to fine work with thinner liquid materials, and bristle brushes for thicker liquid materials. In gilding, round or flat bristle brushes are used for backgrounds. The bristles usually come from domesticated or wild pigs. They are bent in sickle shape and especially stiff and strong. The tips of the bristles separate or split at their ends and this provide an even application of paint. Compared to hair brushes, bristle brushes are generally stiffer and offer more opposition to the paint when painting. Strengths 4, 6, 8 and 10 are used.

The finer hair brushes are likewise used in different strengths for paint application or bole work. These brushes use a set of fine hairs that have a more or les fine point, depending on the type of hair. A hair brush is soft, fine and flexible, and is thus very well suited to thinner liquid materials. They use bear, camel (pony), badger, squirrel, polecat, cattle, red marten, weasel and goat hair. The most expensive and highly valued types of brushes are made with marten or badger hair. But squirrel- and cattle-hair brushes are used most often. The fine red marten brushes are especially good for fine work on vessels, and sufficient quantities of strengths 3 to 8 should be kept on hand.

A special brush for the gilder is the so-called turn-in brush (quill brush). These short hair brushes are very soft and are used to rub out or turn in the gold after matte gilding. Here the brush hair is brought together in a feather quill, the size of which can extend from a small pigeon quill to a large swan quill.

In principle, only a few brushes are needed, for good brushes can be cleaned over and over, and used for many different jobs.

Tips

Brushes should never be set on their tips, for the fine hairs will bend or split.

The cleaning of brushes can be done with green or neutral soap and warm water. Oil paints are removed first with artificial turpentine, spirit lacquers with spirits, and nitro lacquers can be removed with nitro thinner. Afterward, brushes are always cleaned with soap and water. A brush is only completely clean when its spray is white again after cleaning. For optimal drying, each brush tip should be wrapped separately in newspaper.

Various Brushes

Left: Striker (bristle brush)

Right, from top to bottom:
On-wood brush (hair brush)
Bole brush (hair brush)
Bristle brush
On-wood brush (hair brush)
2 double-quill brushes (hair brushes)
Stub brush/bole brush (bristle brush)

The Gilding Cushion

The gilding, or gold, cushion is needed to take the gold leaf out of its book and cut it. It consists of a wooden board (25 or 27 x 15 cm) with a frame, a soft padding and a calf- or sheep-leather covering. A windshield of parchment paper can be attached to one edge of the board to allow work without air currents. On the underside are two holding grooves, so that the board can be held better for freehand work.

The gilding cushion serves as a base for work. The individual leaves are cut into suitable pieces on this base, so they can be applied to the object to be gilded with the brush, the "on-shooter". The gilding cushion should always be kept clean and free of grease, so that the gold leaves laid on it do not stick fast. It is cleaned with Vienna chalk, which should be rubbed off carefully with a linen cloth.

The Gilding Knife

The blade of the gilding knife is made of steel and is sharpened on both sides. It is 14 to 15 cm long, 12 or 24 mm wide, and has a rounded point and a wooden handle. The knife is used to cut, raise and smooth the gold leaves on the gilding cushion. The two blades must not be too sharp, since they could otherwise damage the leather of the gilding cushion. The gilding knife should always be clean and free of rust and grease, since the gold leaf would otherwise stick to it or tear. The blade can also be cleaned with Vienna chalk, and should be re-sharpened or drawn over a whetstone from time to time.

The Gilding Brush

The wide, flat brush with which the gold is applied to the surface to be gilded is known as the "on-shooter". It is usually

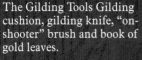

The Gilding Tools Gilding cushion, gilding knife, "on-shooter" brush and book of gold leaves.

made of squirrel hair some 4 to 5 cm long, and is enclosed in a colored box. There are single- and double-strength brushes, the latter for use with silver leaf.

The gold leaf is picked up by the outer points of the brush. If the gold leaf does not stick to the brush by the electrostatic load of the hairs, it usually suffices to run the brush over one's skin. The brush should be cleaned carefully of all bits of gold or grease after using.

The Polishing Stone

In gloss gilding with bole, the last work process before the final lacquering is the polishing of the gold. A polishing stone of agate, attached to a wooden handle with a metal sleeve, is used for this. Agate, a semi-precious stone, is ideal for polishing gold, as it is elastic and can stand much pressure. It is also easy to clean. In early times, a canine tooth of a wild boar or dog was used. Polishing stones are available in many shapes, rounded or curved, ad thus allow gold to be polished on any surface. They are prone to breaking, though, and must therefore be protected from breakage and dirt. One can get by with a few polishing stones, which are best kept safely in a soft cloth purse with individual stepped niches. After long use, the stones become very glossy, and need a new smooth, matte grinding for optimal polishing of gold. The agates can be worked for this use by a gem cutter or be carefully treated with an oilstone.

With these agate polishing stones, the gold is polished carefully on its background with light but steady pressure. Polishing is a matter of experience, for only when a feeling for the delicacy of the work and a light hand are available can one attain a smooth, evenly shining polish of the gold surface.

Various Polishing Stones
For various profiles, there are differently shaped agate polishing stones.

The Material

The structure of a gilding always consists of the foundation, bole or lacquer background, and gold layer. For the individual layers, all the components are applied individually and all foundations are prepared personally. The needed materials are described below.

Materials for Priming

The Adhesives

Glues are the most important organic binding materials used in gilding work. They are used as a surface for attaching all cements, surfaces and bole as backgrounds for the gold. Animal adhesives are used as a binding material for the foundation. A type of adhesive paint is manufactured for this. Basically, all adhesives must be diluted in cold water and then thinned with hot water in a water bath and slowly dissolved.

Various adhesives are used; their common ingredient is gluten. The adhesive strength of this albumen is based on its highly molecular characteristic and its molecular chains. The adhesives are made by cooking out skins and bones. After they are purified, they are cooked in kettles at 90 degrees Celsius, whereby the collagens are released as gluten. The resulting adhesive broth is thickened by steaming and then poured into molds, cut into plates and dried. The adhesives become liquid again when warmed, but they can also be dissolved in water in a dry form.

Finely worked decorations, as on this object, succeed only when the materials used and the foundation are of high quality. Work of Wiebke Schwerdtfeger.

Various adhesives and adhesive qualities are available, and can be divided into skin and bone adhesives. Skin adhesives often have a lighter color, bone adhesives a darker one. The quality of an adhesive is shown by its color and its slow expansion. Good types of adhesive expand very strongly without losing their shape or flowing off.

The bone and pearl adhesives are used to form shapes, for the stone base and for adhesive colors. Their pearl shape is retained by dripping the hot adhesive on hydrocarbons, such as gasoline, where the hot drops instantly harden into pearls.

Rabbit-skin adhesive is made of rabbit pelts and can be bought in plate or granular form. Rabbit adhesive is used mainly for foundations and bole. This adhesive runs well and evenly, can be polished easily, and is rather brittle after drying. Rabbit adhesive in plate form can be used for engraved surfaces and adhesive shapes.

Food gelatine is a very high-quality adhesive, which can be had in powder or leaf form. Gelatine can be used for the bole.

Sturgeon-bladder adhesive is made of the interior of the bladders of sturgeon and other types of such fish, and is the purest, most valued and most expensive type of adhesive. Because of its transparency and great adhesion, it is used in restoration and behind-glass gilding.

A Tip

Various shipments of adhesive can differ in strength and quality, even from the same manufacturer. Thus it is recommended to check the strength and quality of each new shipment by means of new work tests.

Note!

No type of adhesive should be heated too much or cooked, since the gluten would dissolve, destroying the molecular chains, and the adhesive could lose its adhesive power.

Various Adhesives From left to right: Rabbit adhesive, bone adhesive, gelatine, French plate adhesive. The adhesives serve to bind all the subsequent foundations.

Chalk

Chalk is the most important pigment for the adhesive colors used in gilding work and the chalk background that forms the foundation for all polished gloss gilding.

Chalk is calcium carbonate ($CaCO_3$). It originated from the accumulation of the shells of small shellfish, and when the seabed rose on account of tectonic changes, it reached the surface. Depending on the area where it is quarried (today mainly England, Sweden, Denmark, France, Germany and Italy), each of these types of chalk has specific qualities. Most types of chalk contain, besides calcium carbonate, small amounts of clay, silicic acid or iron oxide.

The grayish stone chalk ($CaCO_3$) is actually a ground crystalline limestone of the Jura formation. It is often used in the first foundation layers of for masses of cement. These very hard and stable layers of chalk give the subsequent applications the greatest firmness and provide an optimal bond with the background. At the same time, damaging salts in the wood are neutralized. The stone-chalk ground is applied hot, and bit by bit, with suitable bristle brushes in the first formative layers. Then comes the further buildup with the chalks listed below, making the so-called white ground.

Bologna Chalk ($CaSO_4$) comes from Bologna and is actually nothing else but plaster. It is obtained by repeated grinding and washing. Its light white powder is valued for its ability to be ground, and for its softness, flexibility and filling power for engraving work. Bologna chalk needs a great percentage of adhesion.

Champagne Chalk from the Champagne region of France can be called the only genuine type of chalk that is pulverized or ground by metal brushes without being washed first. This chalk is a very white, heavy, thick powder that brings about a very good formative process but has little filling power. Champagne chalk forms a firm, hard and thick base that can scarcely be ground or engraved. For this reason, this type of chalk is often mixed with others or used for the stable layering of a foundation.

China Clay is a hydrated aluminum silicate (Si_2O_5), and is quarried mainly in southern England. It forms fine flakes and thus looks very greasy, fine, soft, and yellow-tinged. China clay covers very well, runs well, and needs very little adhesive. An adhesive coloring with China clay is superbly suited for figures or find carvings. It can be brushed as a dry coloring paint and is used for white polishing techniques.

Whitening Chalk is quarried as raw chalk, and is a calcium carbonate ($CaCO_3$) that is cleansed of the crudest impurities by washing. It can absorb very much and has a light to white color. For foundations, it is suited only in mixtures with other types of chalk, but can be used very well for shapes and masses of cement.

A Tip

Chalk should be stored dry, since it attracts moisture otherwise and can then form clumps of adhesions.

**Various Clays and Chalks
From top to bottom:** Whitening chalk, stone chalk, Champagne chalk, China clay. The different chalks with their varying qualities serve as pigments, fillers and foundations for the wooden background.

The Bole

Bole is the most important pigment in gilding work. It forms the actual gold background. Bole should always be on hand in the workshop, in small amounts but always in a variety of colors. Little of it is used, and the colors can always be mixed with each other.

Bole is a very fine, sift and sand-free clay, prepared by washing; it produces the background as the actual gold carrier through the addition of grease, wax or tallow. The raw material is provided by a clay silicate and a natural, very greasy, earth pigment. For further use, bole is first cleansed of all coarse and unclean components, to allow optimal polishing of the gold later. The volumes and soft grain assures that the gold leaf applied to it will bond and can be polished to a high gloss with an agate polishing stone. Bole is either dried and available as the classic "cone" or "little hat" or as a moist paste in a variety of colors.

The color of the bole has a decisive effect on the total effect of the gold background, since it shimmers through the thin gold-leaf covering. The traditional, classic colors are red or ochre tones. The yellow or ochre bole is very similar to gold and provides a good transition between gold and background. Traditionally, a red bole is applied to and ochre bole as a last layer, so as to emphasize the glow and glitter of the gold. Red bole was already known in all of Europe in Roman times, and white bole was also typical of Roman-influenced northern Europe. Yellow bole was used later, in the Baroque era of the 17th and 18th centuries.

Today ochre-colored bole is often chosen for matte gilding, while gray, blue, green or black bole is preferred for work with silver or white gold. The modern bole colors extend from red, yellow, green, white, blue, black and gray to old rose, light blue, and signal red.

Boles are bought in these containers and used directly from them.

Bole Colors. Bole is available today in various color shades and qualities. They can be mixed, thus allowing many possible varieties.

Coatings & Lacquers

Lacquers serve to complete most gilding. They form a thin, hard, smooth and water-insoluble layer that hangs together and protects the sensitive gold basis from mechanical damage. At the same time, they prevent the oxidation of the less pure metals, such as silver and white gold.

Oil, resin or alkyd resin lacquers are not used for coating, since they can cause color changes. Yet they are used frequently for outside gilding for foundations on metal surfaces. Natural resins, such as dammar resin or mastix are very rarely used in gilding for binding materials or coating lacquers; they are used mainly in painting and restoration. Acrylic resin lacquers can be used for inside foundations, but not as coatings for gilding.

Shellac is the most traditional natural lacquer for protection and for coloring of gilding. It consists of a substance from the lac beetle of India and Thailand. Stock shellac (raw shellac) is different from leaf shellac. Depending on its additives, different grades of quality also exist. The original shellac is the ruby shellac, dark red in color and leaflike in form. This is always purified and bleached further, and attains various tones and qualities. It ranges from orange through lemon to bleached or blond shellac.

The usual commercial varieties range from large leaves to finely pulverized shellac. The lacquer is soluble in various solvents and is usually dissolved in spirits for gilding, thus as an isolating means or coating lacquer.

Shellac dries very quickly, and much experience and methodology are required before one can apply this lacquer evenly with a brush. Shellac in its various tones can also be used as gold lacquer for coloring gold and silver surfaces. It is not impervious to weather, and should therefore only be used for interior work.

Zapon lacquer is the most modern coating lacquer for gilding, and is one of the nitrocellulose lacquers, which dry especially quickly and evenly. The water-clear film of lacquer is very thin and not very filling. Thus Zapon lacquer is applied easily, does not affect the polished gold surface, and forms a transparent protective layer. This lacquer is not impervious to weather and thus can be used only for interior work.

Applying oil is the real bonding material for matte gilding, and consists of linseed oil containing fixatives. It is long-lasting, and various types with varying drying times should be on hand in small quantities. Applying oil is tough, thick, and dries without sticking in various lengths of time. It contains linseed oil and lead, and thus can be injurious to health if applied incorrectly.

An important quality of applying oil is its tendency to remain sticky indefinitely and thus to hold the gold firmly. The best applying oil has a drying time of twelve hours, but three- and 24-hour oils are also on the market.

An alternative for fast work is gilding milk, an emulsion that dries extremely quickly but keeps its adhesive quality for a long time.

Opposite:
Shellac is available in various types. It is dissolved in various solvents when needed, and can then be used. *From left to right:* ruby shellac (natural) and lemon shellac (bleached) in leaf form.

The applying oil must dry until only a hint of its sticking quality remains, and only then can the gold leaf be applied to the still-sticky oil. The application of the oil should be very thin and done with a dust-free brush. During the drying phase, 3, 12 or 24 hours, the gilded object should be kept as dust-free as possible.

Solvents

Solvents have many tasks: They are used for cleaning, for thinning and dissolving of lacquer or for the "net" in bole gilding. Solvents should be used with great care, for they can be unhealthy if used wrongly. In principle, they should be used only sparingly and in well-ventilated areas. Before you open the wrapper, be sure to note the manufacturer's instructions!

Balsam Oil is a thinner for oily bonding materials such as resins, and for cleaners. In painting and restoration it is often used, and often incorrectly called turpentine. It is a thin, water-clear fluid with a pleasant, aromatic aroma, and is obtained from living coniferous trees by distillation. Turpentine oil thickens in air, and thus should always be stored in closed airtight containers. Being an etheric oil, it is irritating and inflammable.

Test Benzine (or synthetic turpentine) is a low-cost substitute for use as a solvent, and is one of the thinners and solvents that resemble turpentine. It is formed as a waste product in the refining of petroleum. Test benzene is clear, colorless, and often has a penetrating odor. It is used mainly for cleaning brushes and tools that have been befouled by oil paint or lacquer. It is inflammable!

Spirits are the most commonly used solvent. They are denaturized alcohol, usually available in the trade in 90 to 96% form. They are used as a solvent and thinner for shellac and a cleaner for tools with shellac on them. They are inflammable!

Attention!

Store solvents only in small quantities, and only where no foods are kept and children cannot get at them. Use them only in well-ventilated areas. They are inflammable and can explode!

Paint

This section concerns paints as materials. They consist of color pigments that are combined with means of binding or various liquid or paste painting substances. Thus it makes sense to have a wide variety of pigments and coloring materials on hand in the studio.

Pigments are the basic color-giving and visible components of paint. They determine the color, the covering and coloring ability, the light-resistance and the ability to blend with other pigments or binding materials. Pigments are mixed with the most varied binding agents for the various techniques of gilding. They can be of a watery, organic type, as in adhesives or eggs, or inorganic, as in the nitrocellulose lacquers.

Many pigments can be bought already dissolved in binding agents, such as in dispersion paints. Often, though, the gilder mixes the pigments with binding agents personally, such as in the chalk background for creating am adhesive color.

Adhesive colors are the oldest, most traditional organic paints with which the gilder works. They consist of pigment, adhesive, and water as a thinner. They are used mainly in restoration, for chalk backgrounds, linen fabric, [p. 45] picture frames, or in bole. Their great disadvantage is their water-solubility. When they are applied and dried, they can be covered with beeswax or [karnauber] wax.

Oil paints are based on the combination of pigment with oil as a binding agent. They arise from the mixing of coloring particles and dry oils, sometimes with the addition of resin, wax, solvents or [sikkatives]. Fat and thin oil paints are different. Oil paints are characterized by a long drying time, and can yellow in time, depending on the oil binding material used in them. The most important color tones for painting vessels are white, black, ochre, light cadmium red, ultramarine blue, natural umber, burnt sienna and English red.

Dispersion is the separation of a material in a liquid. Depending on the kind of dispersion, dispersion paints can be classified as emulsions and suspensions. In emulsions or oil-bearing dispersions, liquid components such as oil or lacquer are dispersed in a liquid. In suspensions, on the other hand, solid binding agents, such as artificial resins are dispersed in liquids. Most of the dispersions that are presently used consist of artificial resins such as polymers. Dispersion paints can be obtained either white or colorless, and can be colored with various coloring agents. The advantage of dispersion paints is that they can be used indoors or outdoors, and also in moist or busy areas.

Pigments are the components of paints that give them color.

Chapter Three

Techniques of Gilding

Oil Gilding

Oil gilding can be applied to almost all backgrounds, both organic and inorganic surfaces. Unlike high-gloss bole gilding (see pp. 62ff), it is weather-resistant and only of matte luster. Thus it is chosen for especially impressive objects, or those exposed to the weather. The result of oil gilding is always matte gilding, since it is not polished and its glitter is relatively independent of its background. In oil gilding, the gold leaves are laid on a small film of adhesive binding agent in the mixture. Applying the gold leaves is done in the last stage of the unbinding process of the mixture, as soon as the paint still has just minimal adhesive power to hold the gold.

In medieval gilding, fig milk or other oily substances were used as adhesives for the gold. During the Gothic era, matte gilding became less popular than gloss gilding. In the Baroque era, the contrast between matte and gloss gilding was first used deliberately as a style element. The matte gilding often elicited a diffused impression; it can optically erase the borders between colored surfaces, or create good contrasts with colored or high-gloss surfaces.

Today oil gilding is again finding many uses in art, design and interior architecture. Its effect is not only very esthetic, but forms a lasting, noble, warmly shimmering layering for inside and outside uses.

Oil Gilding on Wood

Most oil gilding is done on wood, such as on frames, figures, and other objects. Oil gilding is also often used in classic combinations as a contrast of matte and gloss gilding.

Wood is relatively easy to work as a gilding surface, and can be made into almost any form by hand or with the help of machines. Physically, wood is a complex material, for it can suit itself to moisture in the air and take up moisture in, or give it out from, the empty spaces of its cell walls (hygroscopy).

In the end, the gilding structure depends on the quality of the wood. Spiral grain, splint wood (the outer part of the trunk), or wood damaged by fungus or insects, and types of wood with oily or waxy contents, thus should not be used for gilding. The wood should be seasoned or dried well before being worked.

Any oil gilding requires a fully closed, not sucking foundation. This must first be prepared with the help of oil-paint layers or alkyd-resin lacquers. For this, the raw wood should be ground, grounded, finely grounded, pre-lacquered and then lacquered. Any color can be chosen for the background, but particularly ochre, since this forms good transitions to the gold tones. In general, the higher the gloss of the background is, the higher is also the gloss of the later gilding.

After a sufficient drying phase for the lacquer undercoat, the actual gilding begins, and the mixture can be applied. The mixture is a very durable standing lacquer, which may need to be thinned somewhat with artificial turpentine and, colored with oil pigments, applied with a bristle brush. In principle, more surface should never be covered with mixture than can be gilded in one motion. Work should also be done from above to below, so the mixture cannot run onto already gilded areas. After the proper drying time, the gold leaf can be applied to the still-moist mixture surface. For this, the gold leaf is cut into the right-sized pieces with the gilding knife on the gilding cushion and placed on the surface with the applier (see p. 34). The gold leaves should be applied as smoothly as possible, regularly and slightly overlapping, so as to attain an even appearance of the gilding. If the mixture is too fresh, the gold leaf will sink into the background. The gilding will then look dull, glossless or wrinkled. But if the maximum drying time is exceeded, the gold can no longer adhere to the background properly. A test on comparable surfaces can be very practical here.

After applying, the gold is rubbed carefully with some lint-free cotton wadding and a cleaning brush, such as a quill brush, and polished again. After its final drying, the surface can be finished by lacquering.

In the combination of matte and gloss gilding of an object, the gloss gilding is done first; only then is the matte gilding done with applying oil.

Left: The capital is lacquered to a high gloss with shellac, and after drying, is carefully painted with attaching oil.

Right: The gold leaf is applied to the prepared background, slightly overlapping.

Above: After the mixture dries, the gold leaf is rubbed with a very fine quill brush and carefully polished. Thus the even, glowing, silky matte tone of the gold leaf is created.

Opposite: Now the polished capital radiates its matte glow.

Shell Gold

So that as little gold as possible is lost in the polishing, the noticeable excess bits of gold are collected in a small box. In the past, a sea shell was used to contain them. This gold was bound with an adhesive mixture and put to use in painting, and was called "shell gold". The leftover bits of gold can also be used to rub gilding again.

A Tip

The brush, the workplace and the object must be made absolutely clean and dust-free before the mixture is applied. Thus at this point one should not dust, open the windows wide, or raise "dust" otherwise. Every bit of dust sticks to the mixture. It cannot be removed, and always remains visible under the layer of gold!

Oil Gilding on Iron

Oil gilding on iron is often used in outside architecture, since it is weather-resistant. Thus, for example, iron fences, shields, sculptures or other architectural elements can be ennobled by gilding. In the sacred realm too, in the interiors of churches, decorative screens or ornaments of gilded iron are often found.

Required for a sturdy gilding on iron is the thorough cleaning and degreasing of the background. Every bit of old paint should be removed from an old iron object, and the new iron object should be thoroughly cleaned. This is done either mechanically, with steel wool, wire brushes or grinders, or in more modern fashion by sandblasting. The depth of the sandblasting should be checked, so as not to remove too much original material.

After thoroughly removing the dust from the iron object, apply a corrosion-protecting undercoat to the surface. Wash-primers, containing zinc dust and available in various colors, offer a good surface for the subsequent paint. After two coats of primer, two or three layers of an oil or alkyd resin paint are applied. For outdoors, a yellow or ochre color is preferred as an undercoat, as it will remain in place of the gold in a long period of bad weather. The individual layers of paint must dry thoroughly and form a smooth, hard and firm surface before the gilding can begin. The surface to be gilded is painted with the mixture, and after the adhesion time of three, six or twelve hours, the gold is applied.

For outdoor use, transfer or storm gold is usually used because of breezes. These gold leaves are attached individually, using sheets of silk paper, to make the process easier. The silk paper projects somewhat on one side and can be held with the fingers. These pieces of silk paper are placed with the gold side on the almost dry mixture and pressed lightly with some lint-free cotton or a soft hair brush. After applying the gold leaf, the silk paper is removed completely. The scraps of gold are kept for future use.

As a rule, the gold is not coated for outdoor use. When 24- or 23.75-karat gold is used, it is scarcely affected chemically or physically by the environment. It should be noted that gilding on iron surfaces is basically not insensitive to abrasion, and thus should be protected from mechanical damage. Coating such gilding with lacquer is usually not practical, as the lacquer would split off or form a coating over the gold in time.

In partial gilding, the gilding is first finished, and only then is the last coat of paint applied. In this way, the gold leaf can be cut precisely and neatly with the brush with the last coat and clearly bordered by the colored area.

Note!

Old orange-colored red-lead paint must be removed, like all other paint. The red lead is very toxic, and gloves and a mask should absolutely be worn while removing it.

Red lead must not come into contact with the gilding, as it blackens it, penetrates the paint layers, and makes the gold look unsightly.

The Angel of Peace by Heinrich Düll, Georg Pezold, and Max Heilmaier, donated by the City of Munich on the 25th anniversary of the Treaty of Versailles (1871), made of gold-plated bronze.

Oil Gilding on Stone

Gilding is often applied to stone, both indoors and outdoors, for example, inscriptions of tombstones, memorial or historical tablets, or modern wall decorations on plaster or other surfaces. The surface may be of natural stone, concrete, marble or cement mortar. Concrete or plaster surfaces usually contain strongly alkaline surfaces or cement contents, and must first be neutralized with fluorates (fluorine silicates, used to protect building materials from weathering).

The decisive factor in gilding a stone surface is the binding of the porous stone material with the foundation of the gilding. With metals or polished hard stone, a firm footing is at hand, but with porous stone, plaster or concrete surfaces, unless the surface is properly treated, any foundation or lacquering would sink in. This would result in irregular or messy edges, so-called oil edges. The foundation must thus be degreased, cleaned and covered with a coating of lacquer in advance.

Preparations for inside and outside use are different. For interiors, the stone surface is isolated for applying the mixture with several coats of thin shellac. Afterward, the gold can also be coated with shellac.

For outdoors, very porous stone should be saturated with bleached linseed oil. Then one can proceed with the application of the mixture. Alternatively, an oil or acrylic resin paint can be applied as a weather-resistant undercoat for the mixture and the gold. Applying the gold is done as on a metal surface. On smaller surfaces, the gold can also be taken directly from the gold book with a brush and applied to the surfaces to be gilded.

After the gilding has dried, cleaning can be done with a piece of sepia (the hard crust of an octopus) that has been smoothed on one side. The parts of the stone surface that are not gilded are rubbed with this piece of sepia and thus rid of brush strokes, spots and any other blemishes.

Opposite:
Fernwärmewerk Spittelau, Vienna This building by Friedensreich Hundertwasser shows oil gilding on concrete and plaster.

Gilding Behind Glass

This technique, which was already known to the Romans in the realm of behind-glass painting, forms a special chapter of gilding. Its high point as a product of the commercial art studios was reached in Europe in the 18th and 19th centuries. Gold was used in religious motifs, used for veneration or votive donations. From the 18th century there also came many behind-class rubbings and portraits of historic heroes, which were made with symbols of honor and ornamental décor. In the 19th century, the development of lithography and oil pressing led to a great competition for behind-glass pictures. Only since the start of the 20th century have they attracted new attention from artists such as Franz Marc, August Macke, Paul Klee and many others.

Today, glass gilding is done only traditionally by illuminators or painters of business signs, advertising or inscriptions, but seldom in connection with the gilder's work. Many behind-glass painters give their pictures a golden background, as in iconic painting. Gilding behind glass can be done with gold, silver or other metals. Glass painting has the advantage of not having the gold leaf on the outside of the glass, which would expose it to weather and dirt. Behind-glass gilding can be done as either matte or gloss gilding.

The composition and quality of the glass surface are of decisive importance. If the glass has uneven areas, bubbles, grains or other inclusions, the gold cannot attain its ultimate effect. Thus very smooth crystal mirror glass is best suited for gilding. It physically enhances the reflection of light from the gold surface and gives it its lovely metallic sheen.

Before gilding, the glass surface should be carefully cleaned, degreased, and washed with glass cleaner or a mixture of chalk and spirits, then dried with a lint-free cloth. The glass surface should not be electrostatically charged.

Matte Gilding Behind Glass

This technique is used chiefly in the creation of inscriptions and advertising signs. As on wood, metal and stone, the mixture is applied thinly on the dust-free glass plate, which has been lacquered two or three times. The lacquered background should have dried well and should be hard. Application is done as in matte gilding. After drying, the gold is polished with lint-free cotton wadding, and it can finally be lacquered with a colorless or ochre lacquer to protect it.

Gloss Gilding Behind Glass

This a rare and very effective kind of gilding, especially in combinations of matte and gloss gilding. It is made with a colorless lime solution from rabbit-bladder lime or gelatine, which is applied to the glass surface as the gold carrier. The strength of the lime should be tested in advance in working tests. In a too-weak lime solution, the gold leaf is rubbed off; in a too-strong solution, ugly coverings form on the gilding. The application is done as in bole gilding, with the gilding cushion. The gold leaf [p. 57] is placed in the damp lime solution. The excess liquid is removed with a blotting-box that is placed on the gilding and carefully pressed by hand. To make the gilding as faultless as possible, the gilding is usually carried out twice in behind-glass work. After the gilding dries, the gold can be covered with a protective layer of clear or ochre-colored oil or acrylic resin lacquer.

Opposite: Venus, Adorned by the Three Graces Copied from Angelika Kauffmann, 1795, 38 x 29 cm. An example of matte and polished behind-glass gilding with watercolor and gouache on opal glass.

Gilding on Paper

The oldest preserved gildings in book illumination go far back to the early Middle Ages. The richly ornamented, adorned and elegant initials used in book illumination, and the manuscripts with gold or silver letter-ing on a purple background, first blossomed in the 6th century, under Emperor Justinian. The "Golden Codices," such as the legendary lives of saints and big pictorial bibles, were often opulent gifts for the sacred or laic upper classes. The gold material had a special meaning here, since it was the imperial color and a symbol of Jesus.

With the rising bourgeoisie, gilding was also used more and more in calendars, chronicles, and finally, sand to this day, also in novels, prose and lyric poetry, and in this realm too, it finally turned from a spiritual symbol into a worldly one.

The technique of gilding on paper has changed little over the centuries. Gilding with a very thinly applied mixture is easy to do. The parts to be gilded are first defined with a shellac solution, then lacquered and finally gilded with leaf metal.

Gloss gilding on paper is very difficult for beginners, because of the very thin layers, since the chalk foundation is not very elastic and the gold adhering to it can break loose very quickly. Thus only paper that will be preserved mainly in a resting position should be gilded in this way.

Book of Kells, "The Four Apostles," © Trinity College, Dublin. Gloss and matte gilding on paper.

Imitation Gold

This kind of gold imitation, with non-genuine gold or brass, is often used to restore old, richly ornamented, historic frames with imitation silver or sheet brass. Sheet metals are used in place of gold, and their effect cannot be compared with the quality of genuine gold-leaf gilding. Sheet brass (beaten metal), sheet copper, or sheet aluminum is used. The technique is absolutely identical to the preparation of oil gilding with these materials. These base metals all come in larger sheets of 16 by 16 cm, and can be had in the trade in packages of 500 sheets. The individual sheets are beaten less thinly, so that they can be held in the fingers. This makes the work much easier for a beginner. But the metals do not have the noble glow of precious metals, and must be covered with lacquer to protect them from oxidation when the work is finished.

A Choice of Sheet Metals
From left to right, in the books, silver, copper, platinum, white gold, and orange gold. Upper center: Beaten metal (sheet brass).

For imitation gold, the lacquered surface is first treated with an attaching oil. The metal sheets can be cut to the desired size with sharply-ground gilding scissors or shears. They are then applied on the background, whether with a gilding cushion or by hand, as soon as the attaching oil attains the right degree of dryness. The metal should be placed on the surface as smoothly as possible, since a strong buildup of grease on the background would become visible later.

After covering the entire surface, the metal is polished thoroughly on the background with lint-free cotton wadding or cloth. This achieves optimal adhesion of the metal to the background, and small wrinkles can be polished out in this way.

When the piece has dried thoroughly and has been carefully rid of all superfluous bits of metal, it is covered with a spirit lacquer such as shellac. Finally, patina treatment can be done; this very easily gives the object an antique effect. It creates the effect of ancient gold-leaf gilding, and a layman can scarcely tell this from actual gilding.

Opposite: Details of the restored frame.

Restored Frames *Left:* late 19th century, sheet brass/oil gilding; right: early 19th century, real gold/bole and matte gilding.

Bole Gilding

The classic bole gilding (gloss gilding) is the highest level of gilding. It is the oldest and most versatile technique of gilding. The name "bole gilding" refers to the actual gold background or carrier, the bole. This greasy clay silicate is very absorbent and at the same time very elastic. Thus the gold leaf adheres to the background and can be polished to a high gloss with an agate stone.

The disadvantage of bole gilding is that it can be used only in dry interior areas and on dry surfaces. The foundation and the resulting layers are water-soluble adhesive paints [p. 63] and not resistant to moisture. The classic bole gilding, which was already used unchanged in ancient Egypt, thus is inferior to the widespread modern oil-gilding.

Bole gilding is very laborious and demands not only much patience, but also the most careful and neat procedure with workplace and materials, plus very careful preparation. A good bole gilding requires much experience and knowledge of the material and background. Even experienced specialists do not always succeed in making such gildings in equally high quality, for work with organic materials is always very risky and often incalculable. Differences in the quality of the materials, the room

The Layered Buildup of Gilding 1) Foundation with chalk surface, 2) foundation ground smooth, 3) applied bole, 4) polished gold-leaf gilding, rubbed off again in the upper area for antique effect.

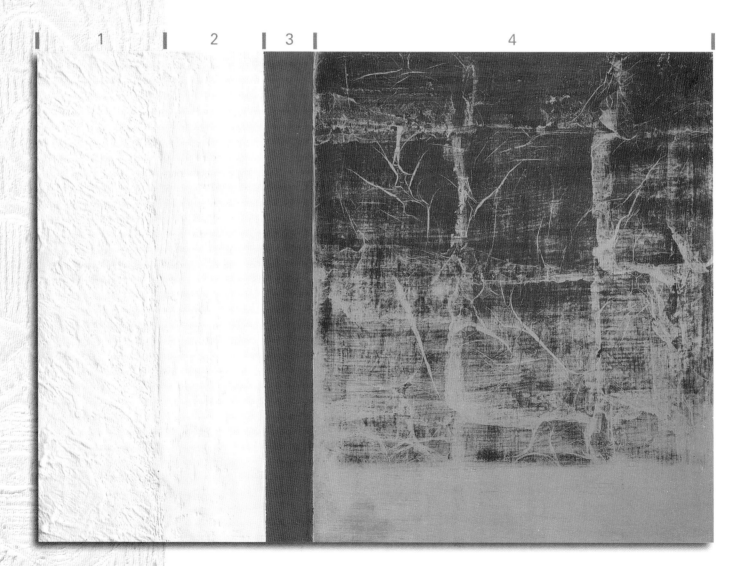

1   2   3   4

temperature and humidity (in principle, as constant a humidity in the sir is to be striven for), plus the laborious layered structuring create difficulties. Thus tests should always be made.

Gloss gilding requires a clean, fine-grained background of even hardness, to which the gold leaf can adhere well. This prepared background must have no unevenness, for polished gold leaf makes every irregularity visible.

Note!

This gilding technique is scarcely suitable for beginners, since thorough knowledge and experience in working with the sensitive materials are required. Thus beginners should start with oil gilding, in order to develop their own routine with the gold and the gilding tools.

The Workplace and Basic Equipment

The workplace should be light and roomy and offer freedom of movement. A table that is stable and accessible from all sides is optimal. There should also be enough space to put the finished objects aside for drying.

A water source and an electric stove or cooker should also be at hand. A professional lime cooker (available as carpenters' supplies) with an integrated water bath can also be used.

Basic Equipment for Gloss Gilding

Materials	Tools
• Bone glue, skin or rabbit glue, gelatine	• Hair brushes and cloths
• Chalks, such as stone or cleansing chalk, China clay, Bolognese chalk and champagne chalk	• Sieve (fine-gauge metal sieve)
• Bole, wet or is cap form, in desired colors.	• Grinding tools
• Solvents	• Clean, heat-resistant containers
• Paints	• Possibly a marble or glass plate for rubbing in bole
• Lacquers	• Gilding tools (applier, gilding cushion, gilding knives)
• Gold-leaf book	• Polishing stones.

The Steps of Bole Gilding

The Wooden Background

Wood is the primary background for glowing gloss gold-leaf gilding. If an object is to be restored, one must find out what kind of wood was used to make it. Wood is basically either heartwood or sapwood. Heartwood is the inner part of the tree trunk, which is especially dark, firm and resistant. Sapwood is the outer part of the trunk. This wood is usually soft, rich in sap, goes through big changes in its moisture levels, and is very sensitive to damage from insect pests. There are trees that consist only of sapwood, such as the birch, alder or beech.

The raw wooden object or the molding should be thoroughly dried before being worked. Wood is hygroscopic, meaning that a shrinking process sets in during drying. During the drying, the wood wrinkles and forms cracks. This can cause finished parts

of the foundation to break off the still-moist wood. In addition, the raw wood should be well prepared, meaning smoothed and finely sanded. All knots or resin must be cut out completely and the spots filled with wood putty.

The Foundation

The foundation forms a smooth and even surface for the gilding. The foundation consists of a, adhesive paint, its buildup and application depending on its further working:

Coating with adhesive creates a surface for the following layers of the foundation. The whole object to be gilded is painted with a warm adhesive solution. The concentration of the adhesive in the water solution depends on the kind of wood. A stronger adhesive solution is used on soft wood than on hardwood. As a rule, an adhesive solution has the right strength when it does not stand glossily on the wooden surface, but takes on a silky semi-gloss look.

After the adhesive solution dries, the chalk base, a mixture of chalk and gluten adhesive, is applied (see p. 36). The number of coats, and thus the thickness of the chalk base, depends on the surface structure of the wood and the further working of the chalk base: If decorative techniques such as engraving or chasing are to be applied, a thick foundation is called for. In principle, at least six to eight coats of chalk base should be applied.

The chalk base can be made with various chalks, which can be mixed. It is recommended that one make tests with the stone base and white base.

The Foundation is made with a chalk suitable for the surface, skin adhesive and water.

Opposite: Detail of a patinaed and antiqued oil gilding with striking metal.

For the chalk base, the sieved chalk is slowly and carefully added to the adhesive taken from the water bath. This process is finished and the foundation satiated when the chalk no longer sinks in, but remains on the adhesive as a small point. The finished chalk base is left standing for a time and then carefully put through a very fine metal sieve.

The finished chalk base is then put back in the water bath and applied warm, layer by layer, on the wooden surface with a hair brush. The surface, not too strongly warmed, is filled by the first layers and finally completed liquidly. The thickness of the foundation layers should decrease with every coat, and the material should be worked quickly. Every individual coat should be dried before the next one is applied.

By constantly being kept warm, the water part of the foundation adhesive evaporates and must be re-supplied. Of course the water proportion should never become too great, since the foundation will otherwise lose its adhesion, and these layers will come off later. After finishing the foundation work, the piece must dry very thoroughly.

The stone base of stone chalk and adhesive paint creates a firm and sturdy basis for the following chalk layers. For it, stone chalk is mixed with adhesive and applied with a bristle brush. As a separate stone-chalk base, it is applied to the dried adhesive solution once or twice, and forms an especially hard and tenacious background for the following white ground layers. After drying, the actual application of the white ground is done. Here a test should be made at first.

With the help of the white ground, a fine, supple background is created, which allows a subsequent smoothing of the gold or the paint to a high gloss. The making of the white ground is done with light-colored chalk. The most frequent gildings are done on mixtures of Bologna and Champagne chalk.

Note!

When wood is used, bubbles can arise and remain visible on the treated surface after drying. Thus one should not "stir around" the foundation.

The chalk base is applied to the wooden surface in several coats. The work should be done quickly, as the chalk will stick otherwise.

Opposite: A Renaissance-style flat frame with bole gilding and rubbing technique.

Working the Chalk Base

By smoothing or repairing, the chalk base attains the desired smoothness. All errors and uneven spots that could no longer be removed later are eliminated now. The most important and laborious work for a good gilding is the smoothing!

In earlier times, smoothing was done with fish skin, sepia bone meal, or plants such as horsetail or especially saw-grass. The widespread "sawing" or smoothing with saw-grass, which contains silicic acid, is no longer customary. Instead, sandpaper is used for moist and dry smoothing. Dry sanding of the chalk base is usually done with flint-paper or sandpaper with a grain of at least P220. Damp sanding is done with lint-free and good moisture-holding fabrics, such as calico or linen cloths, or alternatively with damp sandpaper with a grain of at least P360. A natural or synthetic pumice-stone is also an alternative.

First comes the damp sanding, whereby the damp parts of the background must never soften. After that, the very fine dry sanding is done. First the coarser, then the finer grains of sandpaper are used. The background must never be sanded through,

meaning that the wood must never become visible in the sanding process. This calls for sensible procedure and even pressure on the sandpaper. One should keep an eye particularly on the corners, since the chalk base is thinnest there. A sanding block cut to a certain size, around which the sandpaper can be wrapped, is very helpful when sanding. Then every bit of the sanding dust is removed with a clean broom, dusting brush or compressed air.

Now comes the slaking. Through the sanding and working, adhesive has been removed from the chalk base and the absorbing ability of the background is no longer unified. To create a good, evenly absorbing adhesive base for the bole, the chalk base is "slaked." The adhesive solution consists of glue for the foundation, mixed with plenty of water. It is sieved, put into a clean container, and applied hot and quickly with a soft hair brush.

To be sure of covering every part of the background, the glue solution can be colored with some yellow or red bole. In this way, the thickness of the painted-on layer even becomes visible, since the solution must never form layers or remain on the object in drips. The thickness of the glue solution depends on the background, since the sucking ability can change from one object to another. Tests are thus very helpful.

Sanding the chalk base is first done damp, then with finer and finer dry sandpaper.

Opposite: A bole-gilded capital in detail. It shows the fineness of the gilded background. The work is by Wiebke Schwerdtfeger.

Applying the Bole

The decisive role in gloss gilding is that of the bole as the actual carrier of the gold. Bole is a clay silicate; through its greasiness and sucking power, the gold leaf sticks to the object. Bole is available in the trade in various colors and in a very fine, pure form. The prepared material is available either purified and dried or in a moist form.

Dried bole is usually available in brick or cap form, and is not yet ready to use. Before being used, the material must first be broken into small pieces and "swamped" in distilled water for about two weeks. This bole is then sieved through a very fine bole sieve, so as to remove any last impurities, and then rubbed to a fine state on a marble, glass or Solnhofen (fine limestone) plate. This work step is not necessary with damp bole.

The colors of bole can be mixed with each other, and should be applied according to their desired effect. The prepared bole is added to the adhesive dissolved in the warm water bath and stirred carefully. The finished bole mixture is now painted quickly and evenly onto the object with a fine squirrel-hair or bole brush. No brush marks or puddles may remain on the object. Thus the bole should always be applied as a glaze rather than a coating, since it will break off otherwise, and it is usually applied in four coats. The previous coat must always have dried first. After the last coat of bole, the object must dry in a dust-free place. After that it is rubbed with a lint-free cloth or so-called bole brush and smoothed until is takes on a silky luster. Thus the last fine bits of dust are removed, and the surface must not be touched any more before it is gilded.

A Tip

The boled object must not be touched with the fingers, since grease or sweat would form irreparable blemishes and bare spots on the gold. If the object has to wait a long time before being gilded, it should be covered with a clean, lint-free cloth. It is best only to bole as much surface as can be gilded the same day.

The coat of bole is applied after the adhesive solution has dried and forms the actual gold carrier.

Opposite: A Frame in Renaissance style with bole gilding, decorated and patinaed.

Applying the Gold

A solution serves to moisten the bole base, so as to bind the gold to it. Usually a spirit mixture of water and alcohol is used and mixed in a very clean glass.

The water should be distilled or boiled, since bits of lime leave blemishes on the gold. Good burning spirit can be used as the alcohol. The mixing proportions should be tested, since the necessary proportions depend on the climate, room temperature and bole background, and can vary from equal portions to three parts water.

With the solution brush, a very fine hair brush, the bole is then partly moistened. The adhesive power of the liquid brings about the adhesion of the gold leaf. Applying and gilding are done bit by bit, until the whole surface is finished.

The tools used to apply the gold leaf consists of the traditional gilding tools: the brush, the gilding cushion, and the gilding knife, plus the gold-leaf book. All the tools should be clean and free from grease. The gilding knife should be without edges and backs, and should not be sharpened too much.

The gilding cushion is usually held in the left hand by the big loop attached to the cushion, and the knife stuck into the small loop. The right hand remains free for gilding. The gold-leaf book lying to the left of the cushion is opened carefully. Then the gilding knife is slid under the gold leaf with lots of fingertip feeling, and the knife is lifted slowly and as evenly as possible on the other side of the cushion. If small creases remain in the flat gold leaf, it is very, very carefully smoothed on the gilding cushion. Then the gold leaf is cut precisely into the necessary pieces with the gilding knife.

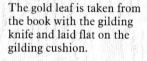

The gold leaf is taken from the book with the gilding knife and laid flat on the gilding cushion.

Then, with the help of the applicator, it is placed on the object to be gilded.

Opposite: Picture frame, early 20th century, bole gilding, engraved and ornamented.

For beginners, these individual pieces should at first be very small, so as to be able to locate them quickly and as accurately as possible in their correct positions on the background to be gilded. The first experiences with this difficult material require very much patience and inner and outer calm. Do not let yourself be depressed by initial errors!

When the gold leaves on the gilding cushion have finally been cut to the needed sizes, the solution is painted fully and evenly on the bole surface.

The gold leaf is then picked up with the help of the applicator brush and laid in the solution. The brush has previously been run across the back of the left hand, so as to achieve a better adherence of the gold leaf to the brush thanks to the skin grease. As soon as the gold leaf is right near the solution, this immediately pulls on the gold leaves, by means of the adhesive power. The gold leaf pieces should overlap just a little on the background.

If small bare spots or folds result, they can be removed by the subsequent polishing. Areas from which gold leaf is missing can be moistened again and fitted with small pieces of gold leaf. If bubbles appear in the gilded surface, they can be pushed down very carefully with the applicator brush. The gold leaf must not be damaged in the process. In principle, first the smooth parts of an object, and only then the decorations and deeper areas, are gilded. The more deeply and sharply any decorations are worked, the smaller the pieces of gold leaf must be to avoid stretching and tearing.

Tips

- ➢ In the workroom there should be, if possible, **no draft;** windows and doors should be closed, and other disturbing factors should be eliminated.
- ➢ The first gold leaves that are taken out of the book usually go to pieces, which fly around the room. This is quite normal, and a beginner should **not be discouraged** by it.
- ➢ Gilding is always done **from the top down,** for the solution must not run into already gilded parts of the object, since irreparable blemishes would appear on the gold surface.

The gold leaf is cut into small pieces with the gilding knife.

Opposite: The small pieces of gold leaf are then placed on the object, slightly overlapping, with the applicator brush.

Polishing

The gold leaf is smoothed by polishing with an agate polishing stone, so as to achieve a firm bond with the background and a shining surface. This step succeeds only when the solution is dry but not dried all through. Depending on the room temperature and relative humidity, this can take two to four hours, and sometimes a good deal longer. The solution applied in the previous step makes sure that the bole and chalk base are still somewhat damp and thus elastic and able to be polished. This is checked with a polishing test of the background. If the gold layer is too damp, the polishing stone breaks in while polishing and ruins the surface. The bole and the gold then get pushed off, and polishing is no longer possible. On the other hand, if the background is too dry, the surface is scratched, the gold becomes streaked or loses its glow.

First the right agate stone for the object or the profile is chosen, meaning that the point of the stone is big or small enough to

The gold-leaf surface appears matte and crinkled before it is polished.

reach all the low spots on the object. Polishing the gold surface is now done carefully, with evenly strong pressure of the stone on the gold surface. Too little pressure cannot create a high gloss, leaving the surface silky-matte. In any case, the surface should look very smooth and highly glossy after being polished with the agate stone.

Polishing requires much sensitivity in working with the background and the gold material. Bad spots or gaps that may occur during the gilding can be improved, or sometimes removed altogether, through polishing.

A Tip

A knocking test on the background with a polishing stone is very helpful in testing the dryness of the background. A dull sound tells of a high degree of moisture, a lighter sound indicates a greater dryness of the gilded surface.

The high spots of raised ornaments are polished first, and then the low areas.

Finishing the Gilding

In lacquering, the finished gold background is covered with a coat of lacquer to protect it from mechanical and chemical reactions.

Zapon lacquer is a very light, clear lacquer which does not change the color or structure of the gold surface and remains practically invisible. Shellac, or spirit lacquer, has its own color and is available in many different shades. Thus the gold tone can be varied in many ways.

When the gilding is finished and all the loose bits of gold and dust have been removed thoroughly, the object is evenly and quickly coated with the chosen lacquer. Zapon lacquer is thinner and easier to spread than shellac. Both types are applied with soft hair brushes; quill brushes are helpful here. Shellac forms layers very quickly, and it takes some experience and routine to spread it evenly on a gold surface without buildups.

The room in which the lacquering is done should be dist-free and have a moderate temperature, as the lacquer can be applied best and dries evenly at 20 to 22 degrees C. Both lacquers dry quickly on the surface but take several hours before they can finally be reworked or patinaed.

After the gilding is finished, it can be "rubbed down," meaning that the look of the background is imitated in the course of time. This results in the optical impression of an artificial wearing or aging process of the gold. The gold layer is thus partially removed by mechanical means. This is most often done by carefully rubbing steel wool or wadding, or alternatively with fine-grained pumice, over the gold surface. The residue of the grinding material must be cleaned off carefully before the final lacquering.

A further means of artificial aging is adding a patina to the gilded and lacquered background with glazes. In this way, dirt and dust that seem to be firmly attached to the background are imitated. The grayish- or greenish-brown glaze color is painted onto the well-dried gilding. Depending on the concentration of the glaze, this can imitate strong or mild aging processes. Then the glaze can be removed from the high spots of the gilding, so as to imitate a higher degree of dust in the low spots. The patina made with glaze can be created with various colors, looking like etching or casein coloring.

Patinas are not usually used for outdoors, since the environmental influences will have an effect on the gilded surface anyway in time, creating a natural patina.

After finishing the gilding of an object, it is carefully lacquered with shellac and the patina is spread carefully on the background.

After drying, the patina glaze is applied and slightly removed from the high spots.

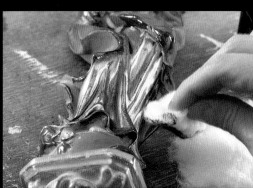

Opposite: The residue of the glaze is then spread with a soft bristle brush.

The Application Base

The application base is a traditional, simple but time-intensive decorating technique. The altar paintings of the Middle Ages have frames or gilded backgrounds that already show this decorative technique in their gilding. In-set gemstones were often imitated by this painting technique.

A chalk base is applied evenly, layer by layer, on the ornament that has been drawn on the object already. In this way, the chosen ornament can be built up three-dimensionally after several coats, and look very profiled. The individual applications should be well dried in advance, so as not to disturb the layers under them. In this way, an ornament can be given several coats of this application base and finally take on a filigreed, three-dimensional plasticity.

After the base has dried completely, the ornament and its background are carefully worked, polished, boled and gilded.

Application Base. After it is careful worked in white, and on a gilded and patinaed surface.

Art Nouveau frame surrounding a lithograph by Theophile-Alexandre Steinlen. Bole gilding with a white-gold application base.

Decorating Techniques

Engraving

The technique of engraving is a highly developed art, and was already used often in Gothic times to decorate altar shrines and apply imitations of fancy brocade or damask patterns to the robes of sculptures. Engraving is the application of deepened decorations to an already smoother chalk base. With the hell of an engraving iron, they are carefully and evenly scratched in, and thus engraved.

In this case, the foundation has to be made two or three layers deeper than in ordinary gilding, and then smoothed very finely, damp and dry. Then an appropriate pattern, with or without rapport (a repeating design), is chosen and fitted to the size of the object. The pattern is then transferred neatly and precisely to [p. 85] the prepared chalk base on the object. It can also be drawn in freehand later with a pencil. Then the ap-

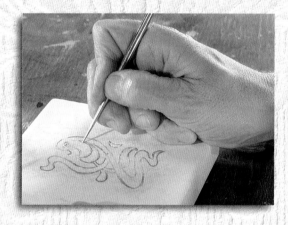

After applying the decoration to the prepared background, it is carefully scratched onto the background with an engraver's needle.

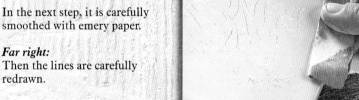

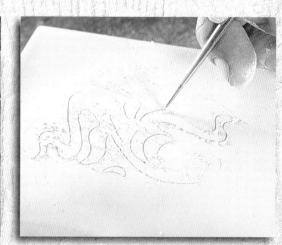

In the next step, it is carefully smoothed with emery paper.

Far right:
Then the lines are carefully redrawn.

propriate size of engraving hook is chosen, and with it the pattern is scratched evenly into the chalk background.

If a three-dimensional piece is to be mounted on a foundation, the appropriate pieces must be carefully filled out with chalk base and shaped carefully into the desired shapes. After the base is engraved, or hatched or quavered, as in the next two sections, it is finely sanded again. All pencil marks, as well as the fine engraving dust, must be removed before the bole is applied and gilding can be continued.

The engraved ornament is applied with bole and prepared for gilding.

Left:
The gilded ornament.

Right:
The gilded ornament is colored with paint.

The finished ornament, enclosed by paint.

Hatching

In the form of hatchings with a row of parallel lines, separate surfaces or fields can be filled out and thus stressed or set off as contrasts to the smooth gold backgrounds. These hatchings are easily constructed background formations and have been very popular since the Baroque era.

Precise workmanship and identical distances between the individual lines are decisive here. For the hatchings, different sizes of engraving hooks, needles and irons are used.

"Verre, violon et papier a musique" (Glass, violin and notebook), Georges Braque, 1912. Oil and charcoal drawing on linen, 64.5 x 91.5 cm. Museum Ludwig, Cologne.

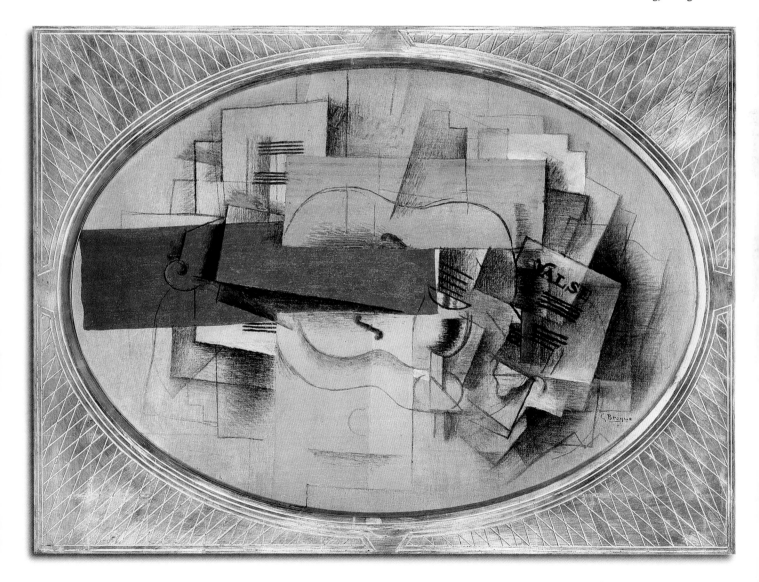

Trembling

Trembling (French *trembler*, to tremble) is a surface formation that has been used since the Gothic gold backgrounds of the 15th century. It was supposed to imitate, for example, the fine textures of textiles or serve to liven the background of a golden surface.

This technique is carried out with a screwdriver-like flat chisel or similar tool, which is quickly and evenly moved left and right over the foundation under light pressure. In this way, a pattern of continuing triangles is formed.

Trembling is carried out with irons of varying sizes.

Bole gilding with Baroque engraving and trembling, made by Wiebke Schwerdtfeger.

Chasing

This decorative technique has been known in Italy since the late Middle Ages, and has been used in depictions of crowns, haloes, clothing, and entire gold backgrounds. This technique can also be found in altar backgrounds, figures or picture frames. The chasing irons that are used have a similar effect to embossing stamps, for they can provide important clues to questions of the dating, attribution and authenticity of paintings or sculptures, since they are made very individually and thus can give specific information as to the origins and manners of production of the objects.

Through the holes made by the process, the light is reflected at different angles, and thus it helps the object d'art achieve a very different, glittering effect. These small punctures, though, are often filled with dirt on old objects, and cannot be recognized any more by their original effect.

Chasing is used almost exclusively on gloss-gilded bole. A negative pattern is attached to the head of a hammer and carefully beaten into the gilding. The ornament is then visible on the background as a positive form. What with the relatively fast wear of the tools, complicated forms cannot last. Today many simple structures can be found on the market: There are hollow punches, lines, holes, rings, balls, mats, and also ornamental punches.

The punches may not have sharp angles. Their punching surface should be rounded, so that the chalk base cannot break out. The gilding must not be completely dried, but should still be elastic. A light hammer is used to do the punching, since too hard a punch would damage the background. Chasing can brighten up a modern gilding of a surface or form a pattern by making rows, repeating or alternating ornaments.

Detail of the Grabow Altar, Master Bertram of Minden, 14th century, Kunsthalle, Hamburg. Gold ground, brocade painting, engravings and decorations in bole gilding on wood. The outer round and rectangular decorations of the frames, as well as the interior lines, are made by the chasing technique.

The Gold Sgraffito Technique or Rubbing

Rubbing first appeared as decoration on a gold background in a 14th-century Madonna picture with angels and saints. This technique has very little in common with the well-known pressing technique of rubbing. The gold sgraffito technique is relatively simple to apply to gold-leaf backgrounds. Its charm is its strong contrast of color and gold, by which the golden surface is livened up. To do it, the gold or metal is covered with a layer of paint. The desired ornament is scratched out of this paint and appears anew in the metal found under the paint.

The interior of the tablet is boleed , plated with platinum metal, and then painted with casein of adhesive paint.

Thus the layer of paint is of decisive importance. The water-soluble paint may not be too thick, for it would come off otherwise. On the other hand, if the paint is too thin, it will not cover the metal sufficiently. Test coatings are very helpful here. Next the chosen ornament is laid out on the dried paint.

A wooden tool, pointed on one side and flattened on the other, is usually used for the rubbing (a slightly pointed brush handle can also be used). With the help of this tool, the laid-out pattern is scraped very carefully out of the layer of paint, and the metal shines through the painted background.

When the paint is thoroughly dry, the ornament is transferred to the tablet and the fine lines copied evenly with a pointed wooden pin or brush handle.

Finally, the completed design can be lacquered or patinaed. Usually, though, it is left with no lacquer and can be protected by a coating of wax.

In this manner, very delicate ornaments, hatchings and drawings, or large-surface scraped designs, can arise on the prepared, polished gold background. Matte gilding is not particularly suitable for this technique, since they can be damaged more quickly.

The finished tablet can then be coated with lacquer or wax for protection.

Opposite: Elegant frame, in detail, an example of the rubbing technique.

Decoration with Three-dimensional Ornaments

Three-dimensional ornaments were often made exclusively by woodcarvers in previous centuries, and thus they were made from wood. More recently, decorations made from elastic plaster, masses of adhesive, or chalk allowed a more practical and economical means of making ornaments compared to the earlier way. A special technique in which these forms were used had decorations attached to frames or furniture in the late Middle Ages. The ornaments were usually colored red, green, or white, and only seldom were gilded. In the Baroque era, three-dimensional ornaments of many kinds were used as added objects of interior decoration, for example on frames or furniture. Since series production was possible, this tradition has lived on to the present-day. There are also outdoor uses, but they are very uncommon, since the decorative pieces are usually water-soluble.

Various classic and modern examples suitable for gilding, made of wood, sulfur, silicon, and plaster.

The traditional gilder, though, also knows several simpler means of attaching certain often-used decorative forms to frames or other objects. In his workshop he has many classic shapes and models, which he often makes himself out of adhesive, wood, sulfur, wax, or plaster. They were shaped after models, and glued to the frame or object, then worked and gilded. The shaped item was essentially made of chalk, cellulose, and adhesive. They were made individually by countless recipes, which differed in every workshop and thus were often kept secret. After they dried, the ornaments were applied, worked finely with engraving hooks, cemented, and then smoothed damp and dried.

To some extent, this technique is still used in traditional gilding workshops or in restoration. Today, though, synthetic resin, metal, or silicon pieces are usually used for these ornamental forms.

A beginner can use ready-made, elastic modeling materials. As an alternative or completion, he can work with classic large or small ready-made profiled wood models, which can be glued firmly to the object.

The ready-made modeling masses as backgrounds for gilding should definitely be tested, as they are marketed in varied forms of composition and quality. In any case, they should be easily smoothed, elastic, and able to be worked very finely, so as to be especially neat, precise shapes, and ornaments. Ready-made types are rarely suitable for polished, gleaming gilding.

Details of a gilded frame with three-dimensional ornaments made from the red silicon mold shown at the left.

There is also the possibility of making free forms independently and gluing them to objects. Large free-standing ornamental pieces should be made with a small interior skeleton of wire or a nail to strengthen and stabilize them.

Finally, the entire piece is thoroughly prepared, smoothed, and boled, in order to be ready for either matte or high-gloss gilding. The foundation and bole of the applied decorations should also be kept in mind so that they are not completely blended with the item's chalk base or bole, but must retain their precise detail. This calls for some work in the utilization of materials and brushes, but saves hours of subsequent smoothing and avoids having the bole layers break off.

Above: **A decorated Baroque-style frame** with pierced corners, smoothed and prepared for gilding.

Opposite: **Detail** of a frame as an example of wax molds of brocade painting, the work of Wiebke Schwerdtfeger.

Chapter Five

Paint & Gold

Paint & Gold for Outdoor Use

Paints are a decisive factor in gilding. They can be used for completion, substitution, or in combination with sheets of metals. Their use can be as varied as the gilding itself.

Architecture reflects the order and characteristics of its epoch and tries to utilize them in esthetic and spiritual forms. In buildings and interior décor, a colorful treatment can change an external appearance extremely. Color used in combination with gold can unite, separate or emphasize architectural concepts or create combinations of structural elements. With the help of gold, simple architectural features can be stressed or upgraded. Gold supports the proportional relationships and heightens the formative and esthetic value of an object.

Paint and gold formations for outdoor use demand not only formative work but also require protection from weather. Countless matte exterior gildings based on a mixture are found in architectural details, such as ornamental railings, church steeples, inscriptions, and emblems, weathervanes, weathercocks, and many ornaments or their parts in façade decoration.

Secession Building, Josef M. Olbrich, 1897-98, Vienna, Friedrichstrasse 12. An example of oil gilding on bronze and plaster.

Paint & Gold for Indoor Use

For interior architecture, the use of gilding techniques is extremely variable and offers a different formative spectrum. Gilding can be applied to moveable furnishings like frames or furniture, in combination with color and form, to set esthetic accents or play a decisive role in architectural formation and its elements in interior spaces. Many decorative architectural pieces, like capitals, borders, columns or permanently installed items such as windows, doors or portals, can be integrated into formative space planning effectively with paint and metal leaf.

The Grabow Altar, left inside wing, (opened), Master Bertram of Minden, 14th century, Kunsthalle, Hamburg. Gold background, engraving, and decorations with bole gilding on wood.

In a **mordant gilding**, the gold leaf is placed in a thickly applied means of attachment, such as that made of warm wax (the "mordant"), and after its attachment, the elegant, three-dimensional matte gilding remained. This gilding is used mainly in churchly and theater painting.

In the course of history, almost all the gilding techniques have been used in interior spaces, including mordant gilding on a wax background, matte gilding on a mixture base, bole gilding on a chalk base and behind-glass gilding. They are enhanced by lacquering techniques and modern wall formation. The alternation of gloss and matte gilding, of various metals in leaf form, such as gold, platinum, silver, brass or copper, on various backgrounds can very much enhance or dominate an interior décor.

The historical development of interior decorating with paint and gold is thus very interesting for our observations. The use of gold and paint in interiors was already known in antiquity, in old Babylon and Egypt. Many royal graves were lavishly furnished with gilded objects and relics that were to accompany the dead king and his retinue on their trip to the next world. The high cultures of Asia and South America also used gold for elegant construction. For the most part, though, gold was used there for sacred or noble objects, and more rarely for interior or wall decorating.

In connection with furnishing a complete room, the development of Christianity played a decisive role. Under Constantine the Great, from the year 313 A.D., elegant sacred structures in Constantinople were furnished in a manner that was to make the "non-material sphere" of these materials impressively visible. The use of gold and glass mosaics allowed a still more elaborate, glowing wall and ceiling formation than in earlier times.

In the early Middle Ages, gilding was often done on white backgrounds, and the interior décor of sacred buildings achieved a new manner of effect by using sculptures, choir cabinets, candelabra, and altar pictures. Wall painting was still usually done without gold at that time. The Gothic era then turned all the components of its structures that reached to the heights, into sacred spiritual concepts. Architecture and painting formed a new unity, and gold was integrated into these interiors elegantly as a symbol of the intangible and godly. The altar, the pictures and sculptures reached their high point. The folding altars, like the one by Master Bertram already shown, presented the high art of painting and gilding. The artists of those times were generally woodcarvers, painters, and gilders simultaneously.

During the early Renaissance in Italy, gilded limestone figures and bronze reliefs prevailed. Wall painting, like book and panel painting, adopted the gilding techniques and used them as a means of illuminating the kingdom of God. The first elegant rooms of the mercantile bourgeoisie then changed gold into a mainly decorative element and liberated it from its clerical dominance. The furnishings of the socially climbing burghers and the patrons of the arts combined gold and paint. At this time, gold was first used to increase the material value of individual objects in interior décor. These artistic-handicraft ideas and the costly materials finally dominated interior decorating in all of Europe.

Opposite: Nymphenburg Castle, Amalienburg, Hall of Mirrors, © Bavarian Administration of State Castles, Gardens, and Lakes. The Hall of Mirrors shows various gilding and decorative techniques in white gold and silver from the Rococo era.

Gilding reached a high point in the Baroque era. The human struggle in the dualism of good and evil was shown in the furnishing of sacred places, in the sculptures as well as the architecture, a transcendental aspect appeared again: Gold and silver should help mankind symbolically in their struggle against evil. This found expression in elegantly decorated and gilded altars, pulpits, cartouches, trimmings, cloth draperies and objects decorated in gold.

The monarchies of Absolutism also used gold as a symbol of their worldly power. Thus the splendid Palace of Versailles built by Louis XIV was seen in all Europe as a model for many patrons of the arts and the artists they hired—and the elegant, solar Aspect of gold became a symbol of Absolutism.

The overloading of the decorative wall coverings and furniture with ornaments and jewelry reached its highest point in the following Rococo. The walls and, in particular, the friezes and stucco decorations offered, in the opinions of the architects of the era, the best possibilities for decoration, most of them being made colorful or gilded. Centering around a focal point in the Baroque was followed in the Rococo by the playful, lilting loosening of all elements of form in interior decorating.

Colorful formations too, like the lustrous creations, took on a new verve through the invention of new color tones, such as Prussian or Parisian blue. The lighting of inside rooms took on a high value; candles and candelabra played a particular role here. Mirror cabinets reflected the richly decorated ornaments and gildings of the mirror frames or the wall decorations and thus created the illusion of an infinite space.

Classicism went back to Greek antiquity and the simplicity and strength of geometrical forms were decisive in architecture and interior decoration. Stencils and reduced-size ornamentation and gilding characterized the indoor areas of this epoch. Toward the end of the 18th century, furniture was often decorated only with colors. Gold was seldom used any more. The ornamentation of these furnishings often resembled fire-gilded cast bronze and contrasted strongly with a white chalk base.

In the Historicism of the 19th century, various styles were combined. The demand for artistic handicrafts for decoration increased, but simultaneously the new industrial production capabilities led to a decrease in high-value artistic handiwork.

Gold decorations are used in a context to increase the material value of an object. Works by Wiebke Schwerdtfeger.

Mirror frame in Classic style, decorated and marble-ized in bole gilding.

In the works of William Morris (1834-1896), gold and glass mosaics and their painting, plus the technique of oil gilding, appeared as manifold formative elements of interior decoration. His style created a renaissance of traditional handcrafting techniques and influenced many subsequent artists.

The return to handicrafts of quality appeared along with the rising Art Nouveau style, in that new floral and naturalistic forms advanced into the focal point of space and architectural formation. New materials, such as iron, bronze, tin, and glass, appeared as formative elements. The material of gold was used mostly for its value as a color when the conception of the interior space allowed it.

In the 20th century, the spread of industrial production, the wartimes and the Bauhaus mindset pushed gold out of creation at first. Only in the seventies and eighties did work with gold and gilding regain influence.

Today is used mainly for decorative accents in inside or outside space formation. Modern design mixes the old and new handcrafting traditions and lets them harmonize playfully or contrast. The combination of natural materials, such as raw wood and precious metal, or the combination of simplicity in form in contrast with the most precious materials, are only a few examples. The manifold nature of these materials comes alive in its formation of interior and exterior space formation in the present very timelessly at present, in a field of tension between tradition and modernity.

Opposite: **"Portrait of Adele Bloch-Bauer I,"** Gustav Klimt, 1907, oil, silver, and gold on linen, 138 x 138 cm, New Gallery, New York.

Right: "Monogold," Yves Klein, 1967, gold leaf and pigments in artificial resin on linen/cardboard, 79 x 56 cm, Museum Ludwig, Cologne. Yves Klein clearly shows the new purism of gold leaf in this gold picture.

An Example of Colorful Creation

The classic variations of colorful creations contain, depending on their style, a certain choice of colors and formation, for example of skin, faces, hands and feet. In the sacred realm in particular, figures, altar parts, or liturgical objects were colored symbolically and stylistically in the style of their times. Today the gilder takes over the work of the object painter.

In this example of a lindenwood angel in Baroque style, the work of the artist is explained and completed. The figure is first finely coated with chalk base and thoroughly smoothed, wet and dry. It is assured that the fine features of the face and the body masses are maintained. The wings are previously matte gilded and lacquered.

For the colorful creation of this figure, casein paint was chosen. The background is first covered in a light flesh tint applied with a hair brush. All colors are applied with different brushes. For the lips, eyes and eyebrows, small red marten brushes are used; for the large surfaces, fine hair brushes.

For the second coat, a covering flesh tone is chosen. The color should not be too pale, and can be mixed individually of white, iron-oxide red, umbra and ochre. This requires some practice, and color tests can be helpful to attain the desired color. This color is applied to the face, ears and neck as well as the rest of the figure, and neatly trimmed. Traces of iron-oxide red are applied to the damp flesh color of the cheeks, the tip of the nose, the chin, elbows, knees and earlobes, and finely dotted or stroked to make the skin color look more natural. The dark hair color is mixed from umbra, ochre, some white and black, and painted on the hair area to meet the skin color of the face.

After the figure is finished, the eyes are formed by precisely applying the white of the eyeballs and the darker color of the iris. The finished figure should be dried thoroughly. Then a patina can be applied and an antique appearance achieved, or the figure can be polished with some wax for protection.

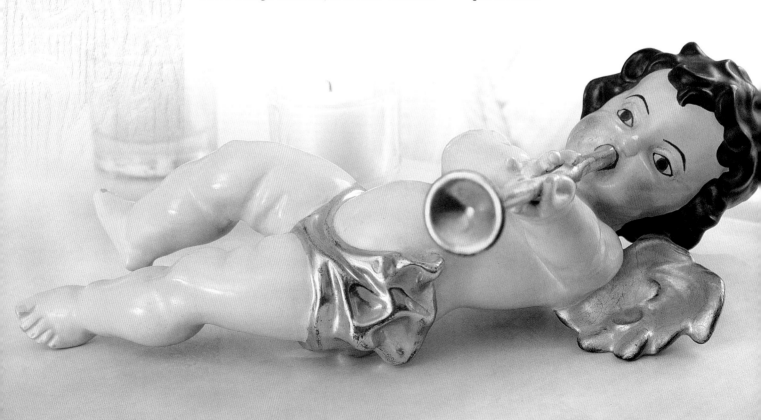

Recipes for Gilding

Recipe for Adhesive and Chalk Base

Materials

- one part skin adhesive
- three to eight parts water
- water bath
- chalk
- sieve
- brush

The necessary amount of skin adhesive is put into the water and allowed to steep; this is best done overnight. The quality of the adhesive can be told by its steeping ability. Then the adhesive is completely dissolved in the water bath. Here one must be sure that the water bath does not exceed the temperature of 70 degrees Celsius, since otherwise the albumen material, gluten, will dissolve in the adhesive and destroy its adhesive power. The chalk is added to the prepared adhesive solution until it remains as a small heap on the adhesive. Finally, this chalk solution is put through a sieve and can quickly be applied as the base with a brush.

The strength of the adhesive differs along with its filling capability and the quality of the various types of chalk. Thus the adhesive proportion can vary from 1:3 to 1:8 parts adhesive to water, and tests of the mixture are absolutely necessary.

Recipe for Bole Adhesive

Materials

- one part skin adhesive
- four to six parts water
- ½ to 1 part bole

The adhesive is dissolved in the water. Bole is added to the warm adhesive solution and stirred. Depending on the type of bole, the finished mixture should drip from the brush in the right consistency. It can then be applied evenly to the smoothed and dust-free chalk base.

Recipe for Alcohol Solution

Materials

- one part pure alcohol
- one to three parts water

The alcohol solution can be prepared in a ratio of 1:1 to 1:3 parts alcohol to water. The mixing conditions depend on the room temperature and the season of the year, and should be tested individually before the alcohol solution is used.

Glossary for Gilding

Absolutism- the form of government, based on monarchy by the grace of God, in the 17th and 18th centuries. (see p. 102)

Adhesives- serve as organic binders for all adhesive finishes (chalk base, bole glue or pigmented adhesive paints). They are dissolved in a water bath and may not cook, as the albumen adhesive gluten would dissolve and the glues would lose their adhesive quality. In gilding, bone and skin adhesives are usually used. (see p. 30, 36f., 44, 56, 64, 107)

Adhesive Paint- paint that consists of *adhesives* and *pigment*. The adhesive paint is water-soluble and is used by the gilder for the finishing of figures, in restoration, for the chalk base and *bole*. For its production, the adhesive is dissolved in a water bath and the pigment is added. (see p. 36ff., 44f., 62, 64ff., 90)

Adicular Frame- This frame was usually formed as an architectural structure of columns, architraves (horizontal beams) and gables, on or over an altar. (see p. 18)

Alcohol solution- This liquid brings about the adhesion of the gold to the background in bole gilding. (see p. 44, 72f.)

Alkalis (lyes)- These are bases in water solutions. They can have strong etching properties, such as etching natron or potash. They do not attack gildings as a rule, but can quickly destroy their backgrounds or lacquers both inside and outside. (see p. 10, 30)

Alkyd Resin- Alkyd resins are thick-oiled polyesters. Alkyd resin or alkyd resin lacquer paints can be used for >foundations as well as advance and covering lacquers on wood, metal and plastics. The danger to health and the fire risk depends on the contained >binders and >solution ingredients. These range from synthetic turpentine to watery >binders. (see p. 42, 48, 52)

Altar Pictures- An altar means in Latin: "Something added to a sacrificial table". An altar picture is a portrayal of adoration of a saint. From this there developed, as of the 14th century, the decorated and gilded wing and wall altars. (see p. 17, 100)

Aqua Regia- This is a mixture of hydrochloric and nitric acid, in which gold dissolves. (see p. 10)

Art Nouveau- This is the French name for an international style trend in the period from 1890 to 1914. In German it was called "Jugendstil," in Austria "Sezessionstil, and in Britain "Modern Style". The trend was a turning away from the historical style of the 19th century. Its artistic handicraft and painting were typified by flowing, surficial and vegetative ornaments. For the first time, it rejected the forms of the traditional frame. Many artists included gold leaf and frames in their works as new formative possibilities. (see p. 2, 24, 26f., 83, 105)

Baroque- The concept comes from the French "baroque" and means "irregular pearl". The era included the 17th and early 18th centuries. Baroque was the art of the counter-reformation and >absolutism. The church and the aristocracy were its most important patrons. It was a time when gilding flourished in interior decoration and frame formation. (see p. 20, 40, 48, 87f., 92, 94, 100ff.)

Biedermeier- A "Biedermeier" is a typical loyal bourgeois citizen. From this concept came the ironic name for the Biedermeier era of 1815 to1848. It was the idealization of bourgeois life and is characterized in interior décor by restrained strength and realistic practicality. Biedermeier frames are mostly simple, light wood frames with black intarsia corners. (see p. 21)

Binder- A binder is a liquid that is either a natural fluid or a solution of solid material. It can come from animal, vegetable, mineral or synthetic sources. A binder dries a finish depending on the temperature, humidity, light and thickness of the coating. (see p. 36f., 42, 44f., 48, 68)

Bladder- The bladder of a sturgeon is used to make the finest, most expensive and best adhesive for restoring or behind-glass gilding. (see p. 37)

Bologna Chalk- This chalk, quarried near Bologna, is soft and elastic, and is used for >engraving techniques. (see p. 38f., 66)

Bole- This concept comes from the Greek "bolos" (a clump of earth). It was originally a red-colored clay that was used as a background for gold because of its greasy, elastic and polishable qualities. This carrier of gold is a greasy clay that can be had commercially in moist or dry form, and in varying qualities. It is prepared as an adhesive paint from skin glue and bole. (see p. 32, 35ff., 40f., 45, 62f., 68ff., 78f., 85, 90, 94)

Capital- This term refers to the closing of a column, pillar or pilaster (including half or pretended columns). Since ancient Greece, Ionic, Doric and Corinthian columns have had different capital forms. (see p. 2, 49ff., 68f., 99)

Chalk- This material is the base of the subsequent layers of gilding. Depending on the further working of the background, various chalks are mixed with each other or worked separately. (see p. 30, 38f., 44, 56, 63ff., 92f.)

Chalk Base- This foundation is made of >chalk and skin adhesive. (see p. 38, 44, 58, 62, 64ff., 76, 82ff., 89, 94, 100ff., 107)

Champagne Chalk- This chalk is quarried in the Champagne region and is light, very pure and hard. Is dissolves very well in watery >binders, but badly in oily ones. In gilding, it is used along with other chalks for tremulous and chasing techniques. (see p. 38f., 63, 66)

Chlorgold- Also called gold chloride, it is a solution of gold in >aqua regia. (see p. 10)

Classicism- This style trend of the period from 1750 to 1830 used antique or Greek models. The Empire style of 1804 to 1830 in France, under Napoleon I, dominated this period and inspired fashion, life style and interior decoration all over Europe. (see p. 21, 103)

Cyanide- This is the salt of hydrocyanic acid. (see p. 10)

Dispersion- This concept comes from the Latin "dispergere" (to divide) and refers to the division of a substance in a liquid. It forms >emulsions and >suspensions (oil-free dispersions). They are used in gilding for interior decorating or outdoor work. (see p. 44f.)

Ebenist- An ebenist is an artistic cabinetmaker. His handicraft was named for the ebony wood that was used in intarsia. (see p. 16)

Emulsion- They are oil-holding >dispersions. They feature a fine distribution of liquid >binders such as oil and lacquer in liquids like water. Often emulgators (substances that make the blending of two inherently unmixable fluids possible) are added to make mixing (for example, of oil and water) possible. (see p. 12, 45)

Engraving- Engraving is a decorative technique of gilding. It refers to the scratching in of drawings, lettering, patterns, decorations or ornaments in metal, glass or stone. In gilding, the ornament is transferred to a coated and smoothed surface and scratched into the background with an engraver's hook or needle. (see p. 17, 21ff.)

Flamework- The German "Flammleisten" refers to ornamental work on frames, particular Baroque frames from The Netherlands. (see p. 20)

Foundation- The foundation forms the background for all subsequent layers of the object to be treated. It carries all the following layers and serves to protect the background, as well as an adhering surface. In gilding, lacquer backgrounds (as in matte gilding) or chalk backgrounds (as in bole gilding) are used. (see p. 32, 36ff., 42, 48, 52, 54, 62ff., 82ff., 89ff.)

Galvanizing- Galvanizing aids the electrolytic creation of coatings on metal surfaces. The object to be gilded is hung the cathode (minus) in the solution of a galvanic bath and plated from another metal object, the anode (plus). By an even electric current in the solution, the metal is transferred from the anode to the cathode and coats it. (see p. 26)

Historicism- Historicism flourished circa 1870-1900 and featured a return to historical models, whose variety of form and architecture led to a mixing of style elements from past epochs. Neoromantic, neo-gothic, neo-renaissance and neo-baroque styles resulted. In interior decorating, massive, heavy furniture and frames appeared, as well as a mixing of ornaments of all styles. (see p. 2, 59, 102)

Mixtures- These fluids form the attaching surface for matte gilding. As a rule, they consist of a long-oily standing oil, which loosens after a certain time. Shortly before drying, the gold leaf is applied to the still-damp adhesive surface. The German term is "Mixition".(see p. 42f., 48ff., 98, 100)

Mordant Gilding- In this type of gilding, the gold leaf is placed on the thickly applied coat of mordant and remains in a raised plastic form even after its adhesion. Mordant gilding is used in church and theater painting, with waxes usually used as mordants. They are applied warm and gilded at once. This technique is rarely used in interior decorating on natural stone, adhesive paint, cloth, or in restoration. (see p. 26, 30, 100)

Painting Objects- The German "Fassmalerei" goes back to the old German verb "fassen" (painting of objects). Religious interior decoration in particular offers a wide range of figures, sculptures and frames that can be painted. The professional term "gilder-fass-painter" originates from this tradition. (see p. 13, 16, 26, 45, 100, 106)

Panel Painting- This is painting on flat, solid material such as wood, clay, metal, or linen stretched on a wooden frame. The pictures are usually made in tempera or oil paint. The technique was very important for gilding in the Middle Ages. Many portrayals of saints and altars have painting on a gold background, symbolic of the nobility of divine principles on earth. (see p. 100)

Pigments- Pigments are particles of organic or inorganic origin that are soluble in >binders and >solutions. In gilding, they are used for glazing, in making gold surfaces of figures lustrous, or to color gold lacquers, such as shellac. (see p. 38ff., 44f.)

Pumice- This "Bimsmehl" is a fine, light ground material used for polishing and smoothing, made of pumice (latin "pumex," "lava"). It can be used for rubbing and antiquing gildings. (see p. 78)

Renaissance- This originally French term means "rebirth" and refers to the epoch from 1350 to the mid-15th century. The rediscovery of classic antiquity and the blossoming of the arts, as well as humanism, are identifying marks of this period. Pictures and frames separated, and picture frames developed into independent objects of art. The gilder's craft became independent of that of the painter. (see p. 13, 18, 20, 24, 66f., 70f., 100, 105)

Rococo- This was the later phase of the >Baroque and >absolutism, from 1720 to 1780. The playful, often asymmetrically formed "Rocaille" (sea-shell shape) was its basic motif. Artistic handiwork and commerce developed, frame art and decorated, exuberant interior decoration offered a manifold field for the gilder's art. (see p. 20f., 100f., 102)

Rubbing- This gilding technique, called "Radieren" in German, has been used since the >Renaissance. A bole-gilded surface is covered with an adhesive paint , and the ornamentation is carefully scratched out with a dull, fine-pointed tool. (see p. 56, 90)

Rubbing through- To make a gilding look antique, it can be "rubbed through" with pumice or another smoothing material. Thus the gold is partially removed from the background, similarly to natural wear. (see p. 78)

Shellac- This material comes from the Indian lac beetle and is used in restoration, furniture making and gilding. In many types that vary in color and quality. Shellac is added to alcohol for working and dissolves completely in it after a time. Then it can be used in many ways as a polish, coating or gold lacquer. (see p. 42ff., 49, 54, 58, 60, 78)

Smoothing Materials- These are aids with which a background can be polished or smoothed. They include the plants of antiquity to modern sandpapers of various grains, with which backgrounds can be prepared in various degrees for wet or dry smoothing. (see p. 31, 52, 63, 68, 78)

Solvents- These are inorganic or organic liquids in which other materials dissolve, such as >binders, >pigments and other coloring materials. (see p. 30, 42, 44f., 63)

Suspensions- These are dispersions of artificial resins, in which solid binders (here artificial resins) are mixed very finely in liquids such as water. (see p. 45)

Wash Primer- This is an adhesive background material for metal surfaces, which it protects from corrosion through chemical processes. For outdoor matte gilding it is applied under oil paint as an undercoat and for corrosion protection. (see p. 52)

Zapon Lacquer- This is a clear and thin liquid nitrocellulose lacquer which is used as a coating over gilding. (see p. 42, 78)

Bibliography

Bablick, Michael and Federl, *Siegfried, Das Fachwissen für den Maler und Lackierer*. Cologne, Stam, 1997.

Bruhns, Margarete, *Das Rätsel Farbe*, Stuttgart, P. Reclem, Jr., 1998.

Child, Graham, *World Mirrors 1650-1900*, London, Sotheby Publications, 1990.

Conzen, Friedrich Gerhard and Dietrich, Gerhard, *Bilderrahmen: Stil—Verwendung—Material*, Munich, Keyser, 1983.

Ehlich, Werner, *Bilderrahmen: Von der Antike bis zur Romantik*, Dresden, Verlag der Kunst, 1979.

Grimm, Claus, *Alte Bilderrahmen*, Munich, Callwey, 1979.

Hebing, Cornelius, *Vergolden und Bronzieren: Untergrund, Arbeitstechniken, Werkstoffe. Ein Handbuch für die Praxis*, Munich, Callwey, 1983.

Hartlaub, Gustav Friedrich, *Zauber des Spiegels, Geschchte und Bedeutung des Spiegels in der Kunst*, Munich, Piper, 1951.

Humpl, Ingrid, *Blattgold: Fachwortschatz-Untersuchung zu seiner Herstellung und Verwendung*, Heidelberg, C. Winter, 1990.

Kohler, Reinhard, *Die kunst-Akademie. Faszination Malerei. Handbuch der Kunstpraxis*, Wiesbaden, Englisch Verlag, 2006.

Melchior-Bonnett, Sabine, *Histoire du Miroir*, Paris, Ed. Imago, 1994.

Penny, Nicholas, *Frames*, in Pocket Guide Series, London, National Gallery Publications, 1997.

Roche, Serge; Courage, Germain; and Devinoy, Pierre, *Spiegel*, Tübingen. E. Wasmuth, 1985.

Sauer, Michael, *Alte Rahmen—neue Sicht* (published for the "Alte Rahmen—neue Sicht" exposition in the Hamburger Kunsthalle, April 30-July 30, 2000), Hamburg, 2000.

Taubert, Johannes, *Farbige Skulpturen: Bedeutung, Fassung, Restaurierung*, Munich, Callwey, 1983.

Wehlte, Kurt, *Werkstoffe und Techniken der Malerei, mit einem Anhang über Farbenlehre*, Ravensburg, Maier, 1990.

Wulff, Heinrich, *Grosse Farbwarenkunde*, Cologne-Braunsfeld, R. Müller, 1979.